New Zealand *food*
and how to cook it

David Burton
Illustrated by
Judy Lambert

David Bateman

First published in 1991 by
David Bateman Ltd, 'Golden Heights',
32-34 View Road, Glenfield,
Auckland, New Zealand.

ISBN 1 86953 066 7

Designed by Judy Lambert
Typeset by Typocrafters, Auckland
Printed by Colorcraft

Contents

Introduction

Traditional New Zealand cookery, if it is acknowledged to exist at all, is often maligned as shamefully dull and incompetent, even by New Zealanders themselves. Not only that, it is supposed to be merely imitative, a poor cousin of British cookery.

Now that is simply not true. As I hope this book will prove, we have a repertoire of national dishes in their own right, quite apart from those which must be considered unique to New Zealand because they use indigenous delicacies such as toheroa, muttonbird or whitebait.

Admittedly, the list of genuine national dishes is small, and easily contained within the scope of this work: toheroa soup, whitebait fritters, curried crayfish, colonial goose, pork bones and puha, pavlova, afghans, anzac biscuits, hokey pokey biscuits, pikelets, belgian biscuits and tararua biscuits. There are, however, literally hundreds of others which can be considered typical of New Zealand cooking despite the fact that they are not recognised as such. No cookery belongs exclusively to any one country, and New Zealand's debt to other cuisines has probably been greater than most. New Zealand cookery is after all, the cookery of immigrants, beginning with the first Maori canoes.

From their east Polynesian homeland of Hawaiki (probably the Society or Marquesas Islands), the Maori brought their knowledge of the earth oven and grilling food over embers, as well as a small number of food plants: the yam, the bottle gourd, the taro, a dwarf type of cabbage tree, and most importantly, the kumara.

In time, the hangi or umu evolved differently from the earth oven of other Pacific peoples, in that water was added and the process became one of steaming rather than baking. Ingenious preparations were developed for such uninviting plants as fernroots and bullrush, and even for toxic berries such as karaka and hinau.

With the introduction of a whole variety of new European plants and animals came a marked change in the traditional eating habits of the Maori. The pig was an instant success, and a method of preserving forest birds in their own fat was adapted to pork. The potato began to take over from the kumara as the staple crop, being far easier to grow. Maize also became popular, and the Maori developed their own methods of raising bread with fermented potatoes, flour and sugar.

While such specialties are still enjoyed by Maori and some Pakeha, there can be little doubt that for the past 150 years New Zealand eating patterns have been most influenced by nineteenth-century immigrants from England, Ireland, Scotland and Wales.

Out of habit, or perhaps homesickness, the first British settlers tried to reproduce the dishes they had cooked in the Old Country. But because they did not have the necessary ingredients or kitchen equipment at hand, they soon discovered this was not always possible. Also, many of the stodgier dishes developed for the icy English winter seemed unsuitable for the milder climate of New Zealand.

However, although familiar ingredients such as flour, rice, sugar, yeast, milk and butter were in short supply, there were other resources instead. The forests teemed with wood pigeons and kaka; the creeks abounded with eels; and the sea shore had paua, pipi, toheroas and other native shellfish. The first European settlers were quick to adapt traditional recipes to these foods.

As the colony became more established, lamb, mutton and dairy products became available in an abundance never enjoyed in the British Isles. Introduced deer, pigs, rabbits and trout began thriving under local conditions and for the first time game came within reach of the common people. On remote sheep stations an interest in the home baking of bread, cakes and biscuits was born of necessity.

Later, in the 1900s, it was discovered that the climate allowed sub-tropical fruits such as kiwifruit and tamarillos to be grown. Beginning in the 1930s, an influx of more sophisticated German Jews and other European immigrants contributed further ideas. To them, New Zealand owes food items taken very much for granted today, such as freshly ground coffee and salami.

Less conspicuous than the wartime refugees, but just as influential on our cooking, were the immigrant Italians and Greeks, nearly all of whom took up occupations connected with food. Those who settled in the Hutt Valley turned to market gardening, while the Italians in Nelson established tomato hothouses or became involved in the fish trade. Many opened eating houses, but the pity was that they were forced to meet the demands of their rigidly conservative market and continue in the rather dull tradition of mixed grills, eggs, steak and chips, tinned spaghetti on toast, and the like. Not until the mid 1970s was the nation ready for restaurants specialising in authentic Greek and Italian food.

What this country has done is to combine all these elements, borrowed or otherwise, into a system of cookery with something of a national flavour. Admittedly this typical New Zealand cuisine was far more easily identified in the 1950s than it is today. Now that New Zealanders are experimenting with other cuisines as they have never before, our food patterns have become blurred.

For all this sophistication, however, there is still much prejudice against our more unusual native foods such as kina and muttonbird. However, since these resources are very limited, perhaps this is just as well.

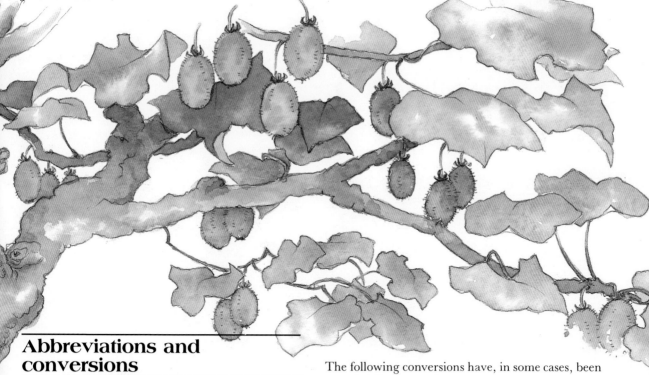

Abbreviations and conversions

The following conversions have, in some cases, been rounded for convenience.

t	teaspoon/s
T	tablespoon/s
ml	millilitre/s
L	litre/s
kg	kilogram/s
g	gram/s
mm	millimetre/s
cm	centimetre/s
C	cup
doz	dozen (12)

Spoons

1 t	5 ml
1 T	15 ml

Cups

1 cup	6 T
4 1/2 cups	1000 ml, 1 L

Ounces/Grams

1 oz	30 g
4 oz	125 g
32 oz	1000 g, 1 kg

5

Maori Cookery

According to Maori legend the foods of New Zealand are gifts of Rangi the Sky Father and Papa the Earth Mother. From Tane come the birds of the forest; from Tangaroa our seafood and fish. From Haumia come the wild edible plants and from Rongo our cultivated vegetables.

There are countless ways of preparing food Maori style, but basically there are only three ways of cooking it. The first involves steaming with hot stones in a subterranean oven called an umu or hangi. This was the preferred method of cooking for groups. For small meals, fish or birds were grilled over the glowing embers of a fire. Boiling food, by dropping a hot stone into a wooden bowl of liquid, was used more rarely.

Making a hangi

Stones. The ideal hangi stones are porous volcanic rocks, about the size of a fist, which are light and easily heated. Next best are the variety of metallic-coloured bluestone found in the Auckland area, or the dense riverbed boulders which are often found in deep mud. Hit each stone with a hammer and select only those which make a deep, ringing sound. Greywacke is also suitable, but mudstone and sandstone are useless and likely to explode when heated. A good idea is to fire the stones beforehand and discard any which crack. In some areas deposits of good hangi stones are rare, and in former times a set of stones was a welcome gift. Some Maori today dispense with stones altogether and use bricks or small lumps of iron instead. Care should be taken that iron does not come into direct contact with the food because of the distinct metallic taste it imparts. Iron should be at the very bottom, covered with bricks or stones.

Wood. If possible, use a dense, quality firewood such as manuka, rata or Australian hardwood. Do not use wood which has been painted or treated, as this may be toxic or taint the food. For the square base of the pit you will need four pieces about 1.2 m long and 10 cm thick.

Food. All types of meat, poultry, fish, shellfish and vegetables can be cooked in the hangi. It is a good idea partially to cook joints of meat in the oven beforehand or to cut them up into smallish pieces. Large, uncooked joints of meat will need 3–4 hours in the hangi.

Peel and salt kumara, potatoes, pumpkin and taro. However, because of the long cooking time a hangi requires, green vegetables such as peas and beans may be boiled separately. If you do use them in the hangi, place them in a flour bag.

Traditionally, birds were stuffed with a hot stone, but the modern practice is to wrap poultry in tinfoil. Shellfish can be cooked in their shells and fish can be wrapped in seaweed, green leaves or tinfoil. Steam puddings can also be cooked in foil or in a bowl tied in a muslin bag.

For a hangi to feed 12 people, allow one leg of mutton or pork, 3 chickens, 6 cleaned fish and 24 each of kumara, potatoes and pieces of pumpkin.

Food baskets. Traditionally, woven flax baskets were used to hold the food together on the stones, but for many years now the Maori have used wire baskets. Baskets allow for easy handling once the hangi has been opened. They can be made by laying out a square sheet of chicken wire and folding up the corners. Use number 8 fencing wire to make the handles. It is best to have one basket for meat, one for kumara, potatoes and so on, and one for green vegetables and fish.

Method. When you have your basic ingredients together, dig a saucer-shaped pit 50 cm deep and 90 cm wide, leaving at least 10 cm clearance for the baskets. Trample the earth flat in the pit and keep the soil in a pile to one side. There should be sufficient stones to fill the pit to ground level.

Put some newspaper in the empty pit and place four large pieces of wood across the pit to form a square. Lay the rest of the wood across the pit in layers at right angles to the one below. Build up to a height of about a metre. The pile should be flat, or even slightly dented, on top to accommodate the stones.

Light the fire from all sides to ensure even burning. It will need to burn for at least one hour. In the meantime prepare the food.

The stones should subside slowly into the ashes, with the heat passing up and around them. They will then be ready when red-hot, with the blackness burned off. Test by flicking a few drops of water over them. If steam rises, more heat is required; if the water runs off in little globules, the stones are hot enough.

The success of this method of heating the stones depends on high-quality, dry firewood, good draught and dry soil. If you have any doubts about these, use the alternative method of pre-heating the stones outside the pit and raking them in when red hot. This keeps ash and charcoal well away from the food. A few stones can be raked on to the top covering of wet sacks to provide 'top heat'.

Otherwise, rake the stones over to one side of the pit and remove all embers and unburnt pieces of wood. Flick the ashes off the stones with a sack, fern leaves or a branch of wet manuka. The more thoroughly you do this, the less the food will retain its smoky flavour when cooked.

Roll the stones back into the pit. Cut open several wet sacks and place them directly on top of the stones. Then place the prepared food baskets, lined with cabbage leaves, on top of the sacks. Place meat in first, then poultry, fish and vegetables. Cover the baskets with clean, damp sacks and fold over the corners of the underlying split sacks so that the baskets are held within a sacking envelope. Cover with more sacks, then shovel the earth over them to cover completely, patting it down firmly to stop steam vents. (If you have pre-heated the stones outside the pit, put a few hot stones on top of the sacking to provide top heat.)

After an hour's cooking, the earth should feel warm, and after 2 hours steam should be percolating through the mound. For moderate-sized hangis (up to 20 people), 2–2½ hours should be sufficient cooking time. Larger hangis will need 3 hours or more — the food can rarely be overcooked. To the early Maori an undercooked hangi was a disgrace, a sure sign of some impending disaster, and to this day it is still regarded as such.

An ingenious method of testing for doneness is to insert a kumara, around which a stout string has been tied, in the centre of the meat basket (preferably within a joint or trussed bird) when preparing the hangi. Lead the string out through the basket and up through the sacks and earth cover. This is easily achieved if a helper keeps the string pulled taut as the hangi is covered in. Pull the string every 15 minutes or so until, after 2–3 hours of cooking, it comes away in your hand. This signifies that sufficient heat has reached the centre of the meat basket to soften the kumara and allow the loop to pass through it.

Scrape away the earth and carefully fold back the sacks to prevent any earth from falling over the food. Remove food baskets and serve as quickly as possible.

On a permanent marae, hangis were dug out of the floor of a cookhouse (kauta), which was usually a simple lean-to shelter but might be a sturdily constructed house (whare umu) with shuttered windows and outlets for smoke. On large, modern marae, the hangi area is sometimes a concrete yard with a circular pit in the middle. This accommodates a galvanised-iron drum which is lowered over the food on the stones.

Bread

While kumara and fernroot formed the chief starch food for the ancient Maori, these staples were replaced in the European contact period by wheat and potatoes. A number of tribes in the Auckland district owned and operated flour mills by the 1860s, and unique Maori bread recipes came into being.

Rewena paraoa (Maori bread)

Rewena (leaven)
2 C flour
3 medium slices potato
1 t sugar

Boil slices of potato with 1 C water until soft. Cool to lukewarm and mix in the flour and sugar to a paste. Cover and stand in a warm place until the mixture has fermented.

Bread
5 C flour
1 t baking soda
1 t salt
rewena (see above)

Sift flour and salt into a bowl and make a well in the centre. Fill with rewena and sprinkle baking soda over the top. Combine and knead mixture for about 10 minutes, adding a little water if the mixture is too firm. Shape into loaves or place mixture in greased loaf tins. Bake at 230°C (450°F) for 45–50 minutes.

Paraoa parai (fried bread)

2 C flour
pinch salt
½ C rewena (see above)
1 t sugar
lard or fat for frying

Mix flour, salt and sugar together. Gradually add the rewena and warm water until the dough takes on the consistency of a scone mixture. Mould into small round cakes and deep fry in hot lard.

These are best eaten with a sweet spread.

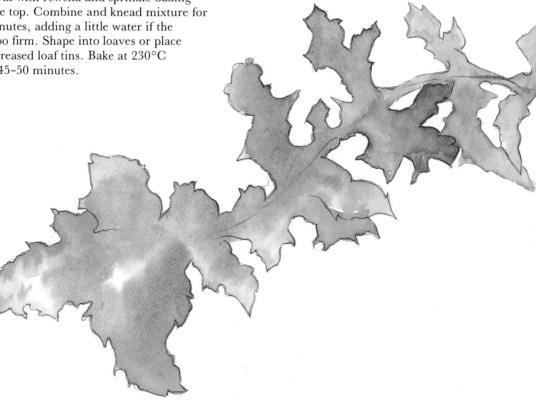

Puha

Puha, also known as sow thistle, is a Maori vegetable delicacy cooked by boiling with meat, usually pork. Probably the best known of all Maori dishes, this can be used as a main meal one night and a soup the next.

Poaka puha (pork bones and puha)

1 kg pork bones
500 g puha

Place the pork bones and puha in water to cover and boil for about 1 hour. Strain and serve the puha and chew the meat off the bones. Reserve a little of the puha and meat for the soup garnish.

Leave the boiled liquid in the refrigerator overnight. Skim the fat off the top and bring to the boil. Add garnish and serve.

Appetisers

As a people with a reputation for enjoying the odd drink or two, New Zealanders are naturally partial to the kind of snack food which mates well with booze.

Peanuts and potato crisps are fine in their place (the public bar of your local pub), but a little more imagination may be needed when serving snacks with pre-dinner drinks to guests at home.

Kumara and pineapple savouries

2 medium kumara
1 X 450 g can pineapple pieces (or 450 g diced fresh pineapple)
4–6 rashers bacon
toothpicks

Parboil kumara whole in their skins. When cool, peel and cut into cubes. Cut bacon into strips and wrap each strip around a cube of kumara and a cube of pineapple. Secure with a toothpick and grill until browned. Serve hot.
Serves 6–8

Blue vein and almond dip

115 g blue vein cheese
15 g butter
2 T mayonnaise
1 T cream or top milk
2 t worcester sauce
¼ C toasted almonds, chopped
pinch paprika

Beat together cheese, butter and mayonnaise. Add cream, worcester sauce and paprika and continue beating until mixture is a smooth consistency. Stir in toasted almonds and chill before serving.

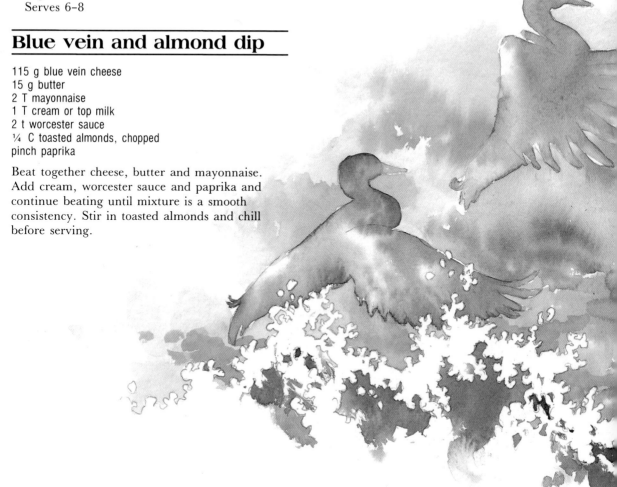

Terrine of wild duck and chicken liver with brandy

The appeal of reducing a wild duck to a paste is that there are no worries about serving up a tough old bird. In this recipe, the duck just needs to be cooked through. The dilution of the duck with chicken livers here will also make it more acceptable to those who find wild duck too rich and pungent.

1 wild duck
350 g chicken livers, trimmed of fat and gristle
1 large onion, diced
100 g butter (preferably clarified)
4 large cloves garlic, chopped
4–5 T brandy
salt and pepper

Cut away the parson's nose from the duck (to remove the sacs of rather vile, pungent oil) and microwave the bird, tightly covered, at a medium setting for 25 minutes (or an hour or so at 150°C or 300°F in a conventional oven). Meanwhile, fry the onion in the butter until transparent but not browned. Add the chicken livers along with the garlic and fry the livers on both sides until barely cooked. The livers should still be pink in the middle.

When the duck is cooked, reserve the pan juices, carefully skimming off and discarding any fat from the surface. Peel the skin off the duck and feed to your cat, who no doubt will be brushing up against your legs by this time.

Strip every last morsel of flesh from the bones, keeping a good look out for shotgun pellets, and place the meat in a food processor along with the pan juices and the brandy. Process on high speed until the flesh is reduced to a smooth paste. Remove and set aside, then add the chicken liver mixture and puree that to a paste also.

Now puree the two pastes together, to mix them well, and add salt and pepper to taste. Transfer the mixture to a terrine dish or bowl. (For a dinner party, individual ramekin dishes are an elegant alternative.) Pour a thin film of clarified butter over the surface. This not only preserves the pate but prevents ugly brown ridges from forming as the pate dries out. A day or two in the fridge improves this pate considerably.

Serve with thin slices of wholemeal toast, cut diagonally into triangles.

13

Soups

Here we find one of New Zealand's greatest contributions to international cuisine — the legendary toheroa soup. While Australia may dispute our claim to pavlova, our ownership of toheroa soup (and for that matter all soups made from unique native shellfish) is beyond question.

The typical everyday New Zealand soup is thick and hearty, full of mutton and nourishing vegetables — a reflection of our cooking's farmhouse heritage. However, only in the winter months does this type of soup really come into its own, and in view of our long hot summers it is surprising that iced soups have only recently begun to take on in New Zealand.

Toheroa

The toheroa is the aristocrat of New Zealand shellfish. A type of enormous clam, growing up to 15 cm in length, it burrows in sand on beaches that are backed by extensive sand dunes.

Its rarity as much as the unique flavour has given the toheroa its legendary reputation, and sadly, it appears that supplies are becoming still scarcer. New Zealand once had three toheroa canneries, but all have long since closed due to a shortage of supply. Ninety Mile Beach, once one of the best for toheroa, now has a minute population in spite of a complete ban on collection since 1971. Only in a few areas is there still a season — and then only for one day a year.

No mechanical aids are allowed in the collection of toheroa. This gives the creature a sporting chance, as you must dig by hand — and very quickly too. The toheroa can use its tongue to dig with amazing speed. At the end of the day during a toheroa open season, the beach resembles a battlefield pocked with shell holes.

Toheroa is both the most celebrated and the rarest of all New Zealand delicacies, said by romantics to have the flavour of oysters fed on asparagus. The more mundane truth is that green plankton, the toheroa's sole food source, gives the soup its rather greenish colour.

The reason for making toheroa into a soup is that the shellfish is rather tough when raw, and needs mincing and cooking to bring out the flavour. Although toheroa is ideally a cream soup without any flesh apparent, many people may consider it wasteful to strain off the precious minced toheroa before adding milk or cream.

Toheroa soup

12 toheroa
900 ml water
1 medium onion, diced
1 t curry powder (optional)
300 ml milk or cream
2 T cornflour
salt and pepper
chopped parsley for garnish

Soak toheroa in seawater for a few hours (or preferably overnight) after collecting, to allow them to expel sand. Open toheroa (this is not difficult since the shell gapes slightly) and mince the flesh or chop it very finely. Place in a tightly covered saucepan with water, onion, and curry powder. Bring to the boil and simmer for 1 hour. Strain (if desired), add milk or cream and bring almost to the boil. Add cornflour made into a paste with a little extra milk, then season to taste. Sprinkle parsley over the top of each bowl before serving.
Serves 4.

Crayfish chowder

A cheat's method this, but very economical if you use the raw, tail-less crayfish bodies which can be bought cheaply at most fish shops.

body and legs of 2 crayfish
1 bay leaf
2 cloves
1 packet onion soup powder
½ C cooked rice
2 t butter
salt and pepper
chopped parsley to garnish

Cover crayfish shells with water and simmer for 10–12 minutes. Strain, return to saucepan and add bay leaf and cloves. Thicken with soup powder blended to a paste with a little water. Add rice and butter. Season to taste and serve with chopped parsley.
Serves 4.

Pumpkin and cheese soup

2 C sliced, raw pumpkin
½ C lentils, washed
4 C stock or water
salt and pepper
90 g cheese, grated

Add pumpkin and lentils to stock or water, bring
to the boil and simmer for 1 hour. Season to taste
with salt and pepper and puree in a blender or
food processor, or press through a sieve. Return
puree to saucepan and reboil. Remove and stir in
grated cheese. Do not reboil.
    Serves 4.

Cold chicken and avocado soup

1 boiling chicken
3 carrots, chopped
3 stalks celery, chopped
3 medium onions, sliced
2 tomatoes, quartered
salt and pepper
1 chicken stock cube
1½ large or 2 small avocados
300 ml cream
pinch cayenne pepper

Place chicken in 1500 ml cold water and slowly
bring to the boil, skimming off surface scum as it
begins to bubble. Add carrots, celery, onions,
tomatoes and stock cube. Skim again if necessary
and season with salt and pepper. Cover and
simmer for 1½–2 hours. Remove chicken (which
should be falling off the bone) and strain stock
through a colander. (Note: this is a basic chicken
stock which can be used for all recipes.) Puree
avocados by pressing through a sieve or mouli, or
by placing in a food processor. Stir in cream and
then add stock. Add cayenne and more salt if
necessary. Place in refrigerator to chill.
    Serves 4.

Seafood

Seafood was a very important traditional food of the Maori. Few species were overlooked: both marine and freshwater fish were caught by a range of methods including lines, traps, spears, pots and nets. The largest nets, called kaharoa, were sometimes more than a kilometre long and made of woven flax fibre. There were special seasons for certain kinds of fish, and strict rituals were often enforced while fishing. Shellfish beds were greatly valued, especially those in sheltered harbours which provided a ready source of food during periods of harsh weather that prevented fishing in the open sea.

Until relatively recently, Pakeha New Zealanders lacked the reverential attitude of the Maori toward seafoods. Early European settlers ate seafood largely from necessity rather than choice, and while toheroa, oysters and scallops were soon accepted as local delicacies, other smaller and more common shellfish are widely regarded as suitable only for an after-match rugby social or a picnic by the beach. Deep-fried with chips used to be the main way of eating fish and shellfish.

However, since the 1970s intense pressure on inshore fisheries has forced up the price of traditional favourites like snapper, blue cod and groper, forcing cooks to investigate the more obscure deep-sea fish like oreo dory, grenadier and the widely acclaimed orange roughy. New Zealand fish is now exported to more than 40 countries.

Oysters

It is not just petty parochialism to claim that New Zealand's Bluff oysters are among the plumpest and juiciest in the world. Along with the nearly identical Chilean oyster, Bluff oysters are a unique species which takes 6–7 years to reach the legal minimum size of 57 mm. Commercial harvesting began in the 1860s, based at the port of Bluff in Foveaux Strait, at the southern end of the South Island. They are also harvested in Tasman Bay.

Our creature has a bizarre sexuality. Most start life as males, but in the next year some of them start to turn into females. By the time the oysters are 3–4 years old, more are female than male. In her new role as mother, an oyster might release 20 million spat (larvae) in a breeding season, though only a tiny percentage of these escape marauding fish and actually get to grow into oysters.

It must be a cold and lonely life down there in the deep for such a blind, deaf and totally defenceless creature which has to contend with many other enemies as well as humans. For a start there are voracious fishes, and the starfish, which wraps its arms around the oyster like some hideous lover, eventually forcing the shells apart and slipping its stomach inside to digest the oyster.

Occasionally, however, the oyster has managed to strike back. One shellfish left overnight on an oyster-opener's bench in 1958 parted its shells. Along came a mouse and, spying a free feed inside the oyster, poked its head in. Wham! went the oyster, clapping its shells shut and killing the mouse as effectively as any trap.

The question now remains as to how to cook an oyster. The conventional wisdom, of course, is that you don't. However, while cooking makes them chewy and less juicy, I feel it also accentuates the flavour.

Oyster loaf

Oyster loaf has had various names including 'Bay of Islands oyster loaf' and 'Tamati Waka Nene'. The latter was coined by New Zealand's most famous chef, Graham Kerr, after a similar New Orleans dish known as La Mediatrice or The Peacemaker, on the grounds that it was the Maori chief Tamati Waka Nene who advised Hone Heke to sign the Treaty of Waitangi. The recipe originally called for a Vienna loaf, but French bread now available in New Zealand cities is better.

1 dozen oysters, in liquor
1 loaf french bread or similar
3 T butter, melted
1 clove garlic, crushed
170 g flour
salt and pepper
1 C mayonnaise
2 t horseradish sauce
1 T chopped parsley

Split loaf open down one side, leaving a hinge along the other side. Scoop out and reserve the soft centre, leaving a 3-cm shell all round. Spread melted butter and garlic around the inside.

Strain off and reserve the oyster liquor. Roll oysters in flour and saute in a little butter for 1 minute. Place oysters in hollow shell and fill almost to the top with the reserved bread soaked in oyster liquor. Replace loaf top, wrap in aluminium foil and bake for 10 minutes at 230°C (450°F). Remove from oven, open and spoon over mixture of mayonnaise and horseradish sauce. Sprinkle with parsley and close lid. Cut into slices and serve while hot.

Serves 6.

Paua

This is New Zealand's meatiest shellfish, growing to nearly 20 cm across. It is also famous for its iridescent shell, much used for ornaments. Pauas are a close relative of the delicacies known in other countries as abalone (North America), buw yu (China), awabi (Japan) and ormer (Channel Islands). Early Pakeha settlers rather aptly called paua 'mutton fish'.

Paua are common around all rocky coasts despite the ravages of poachers who find a ready export market for their pickings. There is still the occasional reef where paua are virtually studded like cobblestones. They need to be prised deftly off the rocks; alert the animal and a minor battle of wills (and strength) will ensue. Once removed from the shell, paua meat needs to be literally beaten to death; otherwise it will be as tough as boot leather when cooked. A gruesome fate certainly, but then the paua has no central nervous system. Properly prepared, it will be so tender it can be cut with a fork.

Fried paua

Remove the flesh by sliding your fingers or thumb down the side of the shell to ease the small oval foot clear. Remove the paua meat, tearing away the soft gonad or pewa (roe). Many people, especially Maori, eat this part but it is rather strong-flavoured.

The paua are then wrapped in cloth (to prevent spatters) and literally beaten to death with a mallet or bottle. No amount of beating will relax muscular tension in a dead paua, so this must be done while the animals are absolutely fresh.

Slice the main part horizontally into two thin steaks and pan-fry for just a couple of minutes per side in butter or oil. Serve with lemon juice and a few grinds of black pepper.

Paua kebabs with tarragon and bacon

Quantities here are flexible. Marinate beaten and sliced paua overnight in equal quantities of olive oil and lemon juice, turning occasionally. Cut the paua into approximately square shapes and slice some bacon rashers into strips. Thread the bacon and paua on to skewers, wrapping the bacon around each paua square down one side only of the kebab. Insert whole tarragon leaves between each square of paua and the strip of bacon. Grill on the barbecue, bacon side down firstly, basting with remaining marinade. The paua will be done as soon as the bacon is cooked. The unlarded side of the paua will then need only the briefest searing to cook it.

Kina

Kina are a species of sea urchin, similar to those found elsewhere in the world, and esteemed by gourmets in Europe and Asia. Common on all New Zealand coasts, they can be found at low tide in rock crevices, and in deeper water, in huge numbers.

The five edible roes are at their sweetest when they are plump and yellow, during the breeding season. Usually this is in spring; when the kowhai tree is in bloom, according to a Maori saying, the roes of the kina will be as golden as its flowers. By the end of summer the roes will have shrivelled and lost their colour, and have a bitter taste.

Cooking kina does little for them; they are at their best eaten raw and preferably straight from the water.

Marinated kina

24 raw kina
1 C sweet chilli sauce
1 T lemon juice
1 t grated onion
1 t horseradish sauce
1 t worcester sauce

With a sharp knife cut through each kina. Remove the roes with a teaspoon and wash well in seawater. Retain the half shells and clean them well. Combine roes with all sauce ingredients and spoon mixture back into shell halves to serve.

Serves 4–6.

Mussels

There are several species of mussels around the coasts of New Zealand. Two of the most common are green-lipped mussels, abundant around the coastline of the North Island, and a smaller, blue-tinged species more common in the South Island. The green-lipped mussels are farmed commercially and can be bought live from many supermarkets.

Mussels with wine and cream

This is almost a meal in itself — a feast of steamed mussels in the shell, followed by a broth which accumulates in the bowl below.

18 mussels
2 T oil
1 T butter
1 small onion, finely chopped
2 cloves garlic, crushed
2 bay leaves
½ t dried oregano
1 T parsley, chopped
½ t ground black pepper
⅔ C dry white wine
⅓ C water
150 ml cream

Scrub the mussels and pull out the beard of each one. In a large pot, heat the oil and butter and fry the onion until translucent. Add the garlic, bay leaves, oregano, parsley, pepper, wine and water. Do not add salt. Bring to the boil, then add the mussels. Pour over the cream and cover the pot tightly. Steam the mussels over a high heat until all have opened, shaking the pot often. Serve in large bowls, shells, juice and all.
　　Serves 2–3.

Fried mussels

20 mussels
1 egg
1 T water
1 C or more oatmeal
fat or oil for frying

Beat together egg and water. Roll mussels in oatmeal, dip in egg mixture, then roll again in oatmeal. Deep fry in hot fat or oil, drain, and serve with Worcester sauce.
　　Serves 4.

Baked mussels

30 large mussels in shell
¾ C white wine or cider

Steam the mussels in wine or cider and remove from the liquor when open. Strain liquor and reserve. Discard one half of each shell, place mussels on a large oven tray and spread each with sauce (recipe below). Sprinkle with a little liquor and place under griller to brown.

Sauce
60 g butter
6 sprigs parsley, finely chopped
2 cloves garlic, crushed
salt and pepper
2 T grated tasty cheese

Combine butter, parsley and garlic. Mix in cheese and season to taste.
　　Serves 4.

Mussel and onion salad

12 cooked mussels
4 lettuce leaves
60 g cheese, grated
6 walnuts, chopped
3 pickled onions, halved
6 spring onions, halved
1 C mayonnaise
1 T worcester sauce

On a large plate arrange six mussels on a bed of lettuce leaves. Combine cheese and walnuts, place a little on each mussel and put remaining mussels on top. Place half a pickled onion on each mussel 'sandwich'. Arrange spring onions, bulb end out, around plate or between lettuce leaves. Serve with mayonnaise mixed with worcester sauce.
　　Serves 6.

Mussel and carrot salad

8 cooked mussels, finely chopped
1 medium onion, finely diced
2 medium carrots, grated
½ C mayonnaise
1 C shredded cabbage
4 lettuce leaves

Combine mussels, onion and carrot with mayonnaise. Arrange a little cabbage in a ring inside each lettuce leaf and spoon over mussel mixture.
　　Serves 4.

Scallops

The New Zealand scallop occurs only in this country but similar species occur all over the world. Scallops throughout New Zealand fluctuate in abundance from year to year, with a boom in catches from Tasman Bay and Golden Bay in the late 1970s followed by a long period of very poor catches. Attempts have been made to enhance these stocks by catching the spat (larvae) in bags suspended from buoys and thus helping them to grow, safe from predators.

Scallops have a unique flavour which is easily drowned by strong accompaniments, and thus are best treated simply, as in the following recipe.

Scallops with raclette sauce

18 scallops
1 C dry white wine
1 T butter
1 T flour
½ C low-fat cream
½ C grated raclette or tasty cheddar cheese

Marinate the scallops in the wine for 3 hours, then gently simmer in the wine for 5 minutes. Do not boil.

Transfer to a bowl. Return the pan to the heat and add the butter. Melt, then add flour. Cook for several minutes then add the wine and cream. Bring to the boil to thicken, then continue to boil and stir until reduced to a consistency thick enough to coat the back of a spoon. Add the scallops, heat through momentarily, then remove from the heat and stir in the cheese until it melts.

Serves 3.

New Zealand scallops

450 g scallops
seasoned flour
30 g butter
2 green peppers, diced
4 spring onions, sliced
1 clove garlic, crushed
60 g mushrooms, sliced
4 tomatoes, peeled and chopped
chopped parsley to garnish

Melt butter in pan and saute green peppers, spring onions and garlic for several minutes. Add mushrooms and cook for 5 minutes more, then add tomatoes and cook for a further 5 minutes. Meanwhile dry the scallops, coat in flour and fry for 5 minutes in a little butter. Cover with the cooked vegetable and sprinkle with chopped parsley.

Serves 4.

Polynesian marinated scallops

Quantities for this Polynesian recipe are flexible. Rinse scallops and finely slice 1–2 onions into rings. Mix scallops and onion rings and marinate for at least 8 hours in lemon or lime juice. Discard three-quarters of the marinade. Finely chop the onion rings, mix with scallops and remaining marinade and cover with coconut cream. Chill well and serve garnished with chopped parsley.

Scallop pie

450 g scallops
75 g butter
1½ C fresh breadcrumbs
1 T flour
½ t dry mustard
1 t curry powder
1 t salt
1 C milk
1 t soya sauce
2 t lemon juice

Melt butter and mix with breadcrumbs. Take out half and reserve remainder. Add flour, mustard, curry powder and salt, then stir in milk. Bring to the boil and simmer for 3 minutes. Add soya sauce and lemon juice and mix in the scallops.

Place in a buttered oven dish and top with reserved breadcrumbs. Bake at 180°C (350°F) for 10–15 minutes.

Serves. 4.

Crayfish

The red crayfish, or koura papatea of the Maori, is a type of lobster found only around New Zealand and southern Australia. It has close relatives in many part of the world where they are variously known as crawfish, kreef, langouste and rock lobster. In fact the name 'rock lobster' is used as a marketing name for exported New Zealand crayfish.

There is a second type of crayfish usually known as the 'packhorse' crayfish because of its large size — up to 20 kg or sometimes even more. Its flesh is denser and less delicate.

Crayfish have not always been the luxury they are today. Before World War II they were not exported, demand on the home market was limited, and so crayfish was a cheap meal.

Traditionally crayfish are boiled and then eaten cold, but cooking them on the barbecue has become increasingly popular in recent years.

Grilled orange-marinated crayfish

Carefully remove the tails from the raw crayfish and marinate them in freshly squeezed orange juice to cover, for 3 hours. Add a little soy sauce, if desired.

Brush the heated barbecue grill with oil (preferably olive oil) and grill the tails for about 4 minutes per side.

Curried crayfish

This dish emerged early this century as a New Zealand specialty and was later recognised as such by the co-principals of the Cordon Bleu Cookery School in London, Rosemary Hulme and Muriel Downes. It is an especially good way of using a less-than-fresh crayfish.

1 medium crayfish, diced
1 medium onion, finely diced
2 T butter
2 T flour
2 t curry powder
pinch nutmeg
450 ml milk
squeeze of lemon

Saute onion in butter to soften, but do not brown. Blend in flour, curry powder and nutmeg and add milk slowly, stirring continuously. Bring to the boil to thicken, then add lemon juice and diced crayfish. Heat through and season to taste. Serve with boiled rice.

Serves 2.

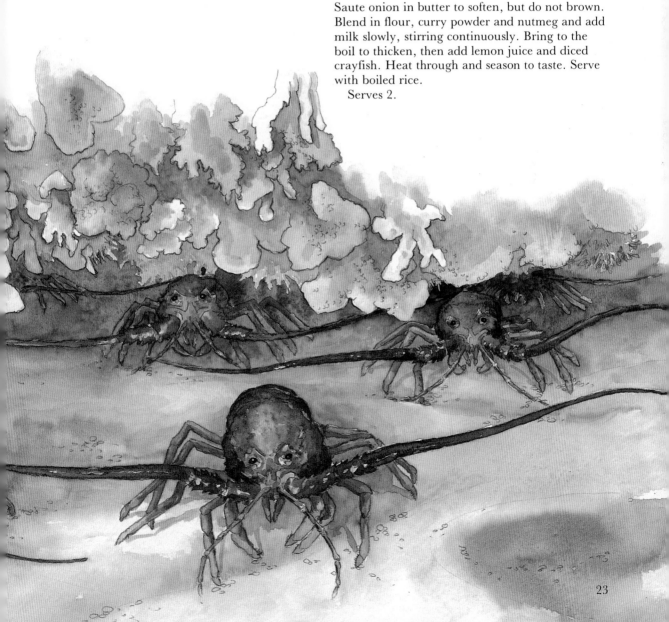

Blue cod

This was possibly the first New Zealand fish to be eaten by westerners: Captain Cook was given some by the Maori, and called them 'coal fish'. They are actually not a true cod at all, but a member of the weever family.

Blue cod are particularly esteemed in southern New Zealand. The flesh is delicate, flaky and very tender, with very little fat. It is quick-cooking and versatile, suitable for baking, steaming and grilling. Smoked blue cod is a national delicacy.

Grilled blue cod in red and green pepper sauce

1 whole blue cod, about 750 g after scaling and gutting
4 red peppers
4 green peppers
6 T olive oil
juice of 1 lemon
salt and pepper

Place the peppers under the grill and cook on all sides until almost covered with black blisters. This will give them a delicious, slightly smoky flavour. Place under running cold water and peel off the blistered skin, then open up the peppers and tear away the seeds and stem end. Cut strips of both red and green peppers and reserve for decoration.

Puree the remaining pepper flesh in a blender or food processor with 3 T of the olive oil and half the lemon juice. Set this red puree aside. Repeat the process with the green peppers to produce a green puree. Season with a little pepper and salt.

Gash the fish with 3 parallel cuts down each side and brush with oil. Grill for 5–6 minutes per side.

Pour the sauces on to a serving platter from opposite ends so they meet in the middle. Place the grilled cod in this and decorate with crosses of the reserved pepper strips.

Serves 4.

Stewart Island blue cod

A lesser-known name for the Bluff oyster is the Stewart Island oyster which, in this dish, combines with the excellent blue cod from the same waters to yield a subtle fusion of both flavours.

500 g blue cod fillets, cubed
6 oysters in liquor, roughly chopped
½ C cream or top milk
¼ t salt
pinch pepper
1 T cornflour
12 grapes, halved

Add water to the oyster liquor to make quantity up to 1 C. Poach fish cubes in this for 5 minutes. Remove fish and keep warm. Add cream, salt and pepper to liquor, mix cornflour with a little milk and pour into liquor to thicken. Bring to the boil slowly, add oysters and cook for a further 1 minute. Pour sauce over fish and garnish with deseeded grapes.

Serves 4.

Ling

An offshore species which is most abundant from
Cook Strait southwards, ling (or hokarari) is a
long, slender fish which weighs up to 15 kg. The
flesh is white and very solid, low in fat and
calories, but rather on the dry side. It is in best
condition in the early winter months and has good
keeping qualities.

Ling is best baked, steamed or poached and
keeps its shape well during cooking. It is less
suitable for frying or grilling. Ling is also
commonly available smoked.

Smoked ling and asparagus pie

This is a good way to stretch a small amount of
fish. In season, fresh asparagus instead of canned
may be used.

300 g smoked ling (or other fish), cubed
120 g butter
120 g flour
600 ml milk
120 g tasty cheese, grated
700 g potatoes
1 x 440-g can asparagus (or 400 g fresh)
1 tomato

Boil and mash potatoes. Melt butter, blend in
flour, add milk and bring to the boil to thicken,
stirring continuously. Add smoked fish and
simmer to heat through. Add grated cheese and
place mixture in a 30-cm baking dish.

Reserve 4 spears of asparagus and mash the rest
in with potato. Spread this mixture over the fish
and score the top with a wet spoon. Bake at 230°C
(450°F) for 15 minutes.

Remove dish from oven and place the reserved
asparagus in a cross on the top. Place under griller
until the potato is golden brown. Garnish the
centre with a fancy-cut tomato.

Serves 4.

Snapper

Snapper, or tamure in Maori, is our most popular fish in parts of the country where it occurs. It is also one of the most plentiful, especially in northern waters. The flesh is fine and delicate with little fat. A very versatile fish, snapper can be baked, steamed, fried or casseroled. It is also delicious eaten cold in salads, and takes to smoking very well.

Urupukapuka fish fingers

A light, genuinely fleshy fish finger with a crisp coating and a hint of coconut.

2 large snapper fillets
2 eggs, beaten
desiccated coconut
cream crackers, crumbled
oil for frying

Cut fillets into even-sized fingers. Dip in beaten egg, then in coconut, then in seasoned cracker crumbs. Fry lightly on both sides in a little oil until golden brown.
    Serves 4.

Opua snapper

2 large snapper fillets, halved
½ C white wine
1 medium onion, roughly chopped
1 medium carrot
½ t salt
3 peppercorns
2 cloves
1 bay leaf
1 sprig parsley
1 sprig thyme
½ C mayonnaise
¼ t hot mustard
½ T chopped parsley
½ T chopped chives

Dilute wine with an equal quantity of water. Simmer the onion, carrot, salt, peppercorns, cloves, bay leaf, parsley and thyme, covered, in the wine for 30–40 minutes. Add fish and simmer for 10–15 minutes longer, without boiling. Allow to cool in liquid. Remove and mask with mayonnaise mixed with mustard, parsley and chives.
    Serves 4.
Variation: Proceed as above, but keep fish warm and lightly heat sauce before serving hot.

Tarakihi

Tarakihi is similar in size to snapper and almost as popular as a food fish. It is high in fat; the flesh is juicy, firm and finely textured. Suitable for all types of cooking, it is particularly good fried as it holds its shape well.

Orange-fried tarakihi

450 g tarakihi fillets
1 orange, peeled and thickly sliced
salt
1 egg, beaten
½ C peanuts, slightly roasted
oil for frying

Rub fish with a slice of orange, sprinkle with salt and dip in beaten egg. Press peanuts firmly into flesh with a spatula. Place fillets in a pan with a little oil, place orange slices on top and fry lightly. Turn, keeping the orange on top of each fillet. Serve immediately.
    Serves 4.

Baked tarakihi with celery and walnuts

4 medium tarakihi fillets
2 T flour
2 T butter
6 sticks celery, chopped
3 T chopped walnuts
1 T flour
salt and pepper
1½ C milk
grated cheese (optional)

Roll fillets in first measure of flour and place in a buttered baking dish. Melt butter in a pan and saute celery lightly for several minutes. Do not brown. Remove celery and place over fish.
    Blend second measure of flour with remaining butter in pan, add milk and bring to the boil, stirring continuously. Add walnuts and season to taste. Pour over fish and top with grated cheese. Bake at 180°C (350°F) for 30 minutes.
    Serves 4.

Trout and salmon

While the phrase 'The Angler's Eldorado' (coined by the American writer Zane Grey) may have become rather worn out in recent years, New Zealand still fits the description. Many lakes and rivers, most notably Lake Taupo, are internationally famous for their brown and rainbow trout. Quinnat salmon are also present in some South Island waters, and although not abundant in the wild they are becoming more available through being farmed. All these fish were introduced last century from the northern hemisphere; New Zealand boasts the southern hemisphere's only wild salmon stock.

Both trout and salmon are rich fish with beautifully pink to orange flesh, suitable for all types of cooking. Trout smoked with manuka (tea tree) sawdust is a New Zealand classic; salmon too is excellent smoked. Salmon has a stronger flavour and more dense texture than trout.

Stuffed trout

This has been recognised by English experts as a New Zealand specialty — perhaps because our trout reach a much larger size and so are more suitable for this kind of treatment!

1 large trout, about 2 kg
½ C sherry
2 T butter
1 small onion, finely diced
90 g fresh breadcrumbs
½ t salt
pinch pepper
½ T chopped parsley
pinch thyme
pinch sage
½ C milk

Make a small incision along the belly of the trout and remove entrails. Wash and dry fish, place in a plastic bag and pour in sherry. Tie up bag and leave in refrigerator overnight.

Melt butter and fry onion until soft but not brown. Combine with breadcrumbs, salt, pepper, parsley, thyme and sage. Add 2 T of the sherry used to marinate the trout. Stuff the gut cavity with this mixture and secure with skewers if you wish (this is not usually necessary.)

Pour milk over the fish and bake in a covered oven dish (or in tinfoil) at 180°C (350°F) for 50-60 minutes. Serve hot or cold.
Serves 4-6.

Baked trout with lemon sauce

1 trout, about 2 kg
salt and pepper
60 g butter
30 g flour
¾ C top milk
¼ C fish stock or liquor from baking
2 egg yolks, lightly beaten
¼ C lemon juice

Gut fish and sprinkle cavity with salt. Leave for about 8 hours if possible. Wrap fish in greaseproof (not waxed) paper, then in several thicknesses of wet newspaper, then in several thicknesses of dry. Place in an oven dish and bake at 180°C (350°F) for 1½–2 hours.

Meanwhile, melt butter in a double boiler and blend in flour. Add milk and stir until mixture comes to the boil. Drop in beaten egg yolks and whisk until sauce thickens. Stir in lemon juice and remove from heat. Unwrap fish (the skin should stick to the paper) and add any remaining liquor to the sauce.

Pour sauce over trout and garnish with slices of lemon. Serve with small boiled potatoes sprinkled with parsley and melted butter and fresh peas or beans.

Serves 4–6.

Barbecued salmon steaks

1 × 2-kg salmon
1 C olive oil
juice of 4–5 lemons
1 t oregano
½ t fennel seeds
1 t chilli powder
1 T chopped parsley
1 t salt

Cut salmon into 4-cm steaks. Combine all remaining ingredients for marinade and stir well. Pour over steaks and leave for at least 30 minutes. Remove from marinade and place over hot charcoal or under griller. Cook for 10 minutes on each side, basting with marinade during cooking.

Serve immediately, garnished with lemon slices or wedges and accompanied by a crisp salad.

Serves 8.

Eel

Freshwater eels used to be one of the most important food sources for the Maori, who called them tuna. Today these eels are also esteemed for their succulence and keeping qualities by the many countries which import them.

The two species — longfinned and shortfinned eels — are much alike, except that their dorsal fins are of different length and longfinned eels grow much larger. Giants of more than 20 kg and over 150 cm have been recorded — among the world's largest freshwater eels. However, the smaller, leaner eels are better for eating.

A young eel can be grilled, fried or baked more or less as it is. However, a large eel is more suited to currying or sousing.

Soused eel

This may be served either hot or cold.

1 eel, approx. 1 kg
1 large onion, finely diced
½ t mixed herbs
½ t turmeric
pinch nutmeg
salt and pepper
vinegar

Cut eel into smallish pieces. Place in an oven dish and sprinkle with mixed herbs, turmeric, nutmeg, salt and pepper. Barely cover with vinegar (or half vinegar, half water if it is to be eaten hot). Cover with a lid and cook for 1 hour at 180°C (350°F).
Serves 4.

Whitebait

The word 'whitebait' is confusing, as there are nearly 100 species around the world and the term means different things to different peoples: in England it is young sprats or herrings; in America, silverside; in Japan, young sea perch.

New Zealanders justifiably claim that their variety — the young of 5 species of so-called native trout or galaxids — is the finest of them all. These are minute, thread-like, quite transparent fish, extremely tender and deliciously flavoured.

Whitebait has not always been the delicacy it is today. Last century it was so plentiful at one time on the west coast that it was used for manure and chicken feed. The Maori, and later the Chinese goldminers, dried excess whitebait by the sackful. This was sent to the Otago goldfields and even exported to China.

Always wash and drain commercially bought whitebait thoroughly before using, for the liquor tends to have a strong, overpowering flavour.

Whitebait fritters

New Zealanders have evolved at least a dozen and a half dishes for their esteemed whitebait, but none comes anywhere near whitebait fritters in popularity. A well-cooked fritter in which the whitebait are infused with a light egg batter is second to none. It is best to forego quantity in order to have fritters in which the batter is just holding the crammed whitebait together.

225 g whitebait
1 T flour
2 eggs, well beaten
butter for frying
lemon wedges to garnish

Put flour, salt and pepper into a bowl and stir in eggs. Mix in whitebait and drop spoonfuls of batter onto a hot buttered pan or griddle. Cook for 1–2 minutes on each side and serve immediately with lemon wedges.
Yields 9–10 fritters.
Variation: Use 3 T dry white breadcrumbs instead of flour.

Meat, Poultry and Game

New Zealanders have always been a carnivorous lot. The early Maori had a hearty appetite for meat, but only with the introduction of European livestock was it satisfied. Early European farmers virtually ate mutton to live, and the country still lives largely by selling it: New Zealand has for years been the world's biggest exporter of sheepmeats, and is also the largest per-capita consumer.

Sheepmeat is still cheap in New Zealand, but it was even cheaper last century before the days of refrigerated exports to the United Kingdom, when a sheep's carcass was worth little more to a wool grazier than the value of its tallow. Even the poorest labourer could afford to eat it every day, and indeed on the early sheep stations it was the staple food for breakfast, lunch and dinner.

'Everlasting mutton; roasted, boiled, or stewed, there was still nothing but mutton,' one early farm-hand complained. Thus the onus was on the cook to try and alleviate the monotony, and it is hardly surprising that New Zealanders have come up with a host of original lamb dishes.

None of these, however, has diminished the popularity of the Sunday roast — plain roast lamb leg or shoulder, accompanied by roast potatoes, kumara, pumpkin, parsnips, green peas and gravy. Traditionally this was served for Sunday lunch, but it is more often eaten in the evening these days. (A hot lunch was traditionally known as 'dinner in the middle of the day'.) The leftover meat goes into sandwiches for lunch the next day, or is eaten with salad in the evening.

Colonial goose

At the altar of homegrown Kiwi cuisines, colonial goose occupies a place almost as elevated as the holiest of holies, pavlova. The fact is, however, that both dishes are not completely original but are more constructions upon an inherited British tradition. The Romans were busily stuffing joints of meat 2000 years ago and took the idea to Britain, where it was popular during the Middle Ages.

A vague antecedent of colonial goose can be seen in a 1712 Scottish recipe in a manuscript book by Lady Castlehill, 'To boil or roast a legge of Mutton', where the mutton is stuffed with mixture of 'sweet herbs', hard-boiled egg yolks and marrow. Furthermore, in *The Compleat Housewife or Accomplish'd Gentlewoman's Companion* of 1753, we read how a leg of veal or lamb may be forced with a mixture of pounded meat and suet, bread, spices and 'sweet herbs'.

So it seems the only unique aspect of colonial goose is its name. The standard Kiwi explanation is that the boned and stuffed leg resembles a goose. However, this is not really satisfactory, for there is no way a leg of lamb looks like a goose, however religiously you follow early recipes, which tell you to stuff and sew up the leg and then 'push with the hands into the shape of a goose', or to bind the leg tightly 'to form a goose's head'.

The whole point of the name, I believe, is that the colonials were using a stuffing which in England had formerly gone into a goose. The cosmetic effects were merely intended to round out the fiction that the mutton was goose. While the list of stuffing ingredients for colonial goose can vary quite widely, the most common is sage, breadcrumbs, suet and onion which, along with minced apple, is the traditional English recipe for goose stuffing.

Supporting this theory is an English recipe for Mock Goose given by Dr Kitchiner in his *Cook's Oracle* of 1817. This is a leg of pork with the aforementioned goose stuffing. And a similar recipe, 'to goosify a shoulder of lamb', is given by Priscilla Haslehurst in her *Housekeeper's Instructor* of 1816.

From 'goosified' lamb and mock goose, it was but a short step to colonial goose. It is not at all surprising that the early settlers regularly felt the need to dress up their monotonous diet of mutton as something else.

1 leg mutton
120 g fresh breadcrumbs
60 g suet
1 large onion, finely diced
1 T chopped parsley
½ t sage
½ t thyme
salt and pepper
1 egg, beaten
milk

Remove the bone by working around it gradually from each end with a thin-bladed knife, taking care not to break the skin. At first you may feel like a surgeon at an army field hospital, but soon you will get the hang of it. (Alternatively, you may be able to have the butcher bone the leg for you.)

Mix together breadcrumbs, suet, onion, parsley, sage and thyme. Season to taste with salt and pepper. Mix in beaten egg and just enough milk to moisten. Stuff the leg cavity and sew up with string. Tie string tightly around the leg end to form a goose's head. Roast at 180°C (350°F) allowing 40 minutes for each 450 grams.

Variation: A shoulder may be substituted for the leg, and variations on the stuffing ingredients are endless. Half a cup of finely diced bacon or ham makes a tasty addition, and the seasonings can be varied by using mixed herbs instead of sage and thyme, or by adding ½ t grated nutmeg and the grated rind of half a lemon. A modern version of the stuffing is as follows:

Serves 4–6.

Apricot and honey stuffing
120 g dried apricots, roughly chopped
120 g fresh breadcrumbs
30 g butter
1 T honey
60 g onion, grated
¼ t thyme
salt and pepper
1 egg, beaten

Mix together apricots and breadcrumbs. Melt butter and honey in a saucepan and add to the mixture together with onion and thyme. Season to taste with salt and pepper and mix in egg.

Pioneer pot roast

Our grandparents would have cooked this in a camp oven over an open fire. Use a heavy-bottomed saucepan with a tight-fitting lid for this modern adaptation.

1 leg lamb, boned
50 g butter or dripping
salt and pepper
sliced onions
sliced potatoes

Melt butter or dripping in a large pot and place in meat. Cook over a very low heat, basting occasionally. Allow 15–20 minutes for each 450 grams.

After 30 minutes place seasoned vegetables under the meat. When cooked, make a gravy from the pan juices.

Serves 4–6.

Colonial drumsticks

Despite the old-fashioned sound of the name, these rather novel and very elegant pastries are probably a modern invention, since sweet corn only became popular in New Zealand after World War II.

8 French (rib) chops
225 g flaky pastry
1 large (450 g) can creamed corn
1 small onion, finely diced
1 clove garlic, crushed
½ t pepper
1 t salt
1 egg, beaten

Roll out the pastry about 1 mm thick. Lay the chops on the pastry and cut around each chop in the shape of a kite which is large enough for one half to be later folded over the chop and form a triangle.

Mix together the creamed corn, diced onion, garlic, salt and pepper. Place a heaped dessertspoon of the mixture on one side of each pastry shape under the chop. Put another dessertspoonful on top of the chop and fold pastry over. Moisten the edges with beaten egg and crimp them together.

Brush with egg and bake for 15 minutes at 230°C (450°F) Reduce temperature to 180°C (350°F) and bake a further 15 minutes.

Serves 4.

Waipura saddle

This is an ideal dinner-party dish for when you are feeling extravagant but lazy. It calls for a whole saddle of lamb and fillet of pork but is easy to prepare, looks impressive and will feed at least 10 people.

1 saddle of lamb, boned and skinned
1 pork fillet
3 T chopped parsley
2 cloves garlic, crushed
salt and pepper

Place the fillet of pork in the crevice left by the removal of the backbone in the saddle of lamb. Spread the parsley and garlic evenly over the meat, sprinkle with salt and pepper, roll up tightly and tie with string.

Roast at 180°C (350°F), allowing 35 minutes per 450 g. Allow to stand 10 minutes before carving. Serve with a gravy made from pan juices, or with apple sauce.

Serves 10.

Maha steak

Maha is the Maori word for satisfied or contented.

450 g chuck steak, diced
3 medium onions, sliced
1 T butter
2 cloves garlic, crushed
2 mint leaves, crushed
½ t ground cumin seed
½ t turmeric
pinch cinnamon
pinch chilli powder
4 peppercorns
4 slices root ginger, chopped
½ t salt
1½ T soya sauce
1 C yoghurt

Fry steak and onion in butter until steak is browned and the onions softened. Add cumin, turmeric, cinnamon, chilli powder, peppercorns and salt. Cover pan with a tightly fitting lid and simmer over a low heat for 1½ hours or until meat is tender. Ten minutes before the end of the cooking, add the garlic, mint and soy sauce. Take the pan from the heat to cool a little. Slowly stir in yoghurt and reheat but do not boil. Serve on a bed of rice.
    Serves 4.

Kumara and prune tzimmes

'Tzimmes' in Hebrew literally means fuss or excitement, but in Jewish cuisine is taken to mean a loose combination of any meat or fruit or vegetables. As Jewish people in this part of the world have realised, our kumara fits this sweet and savoury idea admirably.

1 kg chuck steak or brisket
1 T chicken fat or oil
5 medium kumara, sliced
750 g prunes, pitted
3 medium onions, cut into rings
2 t cinnamon
1½ t salt
½ t pepper
2 t butter
¾ C dark honey or brown sugar

Cut steak into 8 equal portions and brown in hot chicken fat or oil to seal in juices. In an ovenproof dish place alternate layers of kumara, prunes, steak and onions, sprinkling each kumara layer with cinnamon and each meat-and-onion layer with salt and pepper. Finish with a layer of kumara and dot with small pieces of butter. Dissolve honey or sugar in 3 C boiling water and pour over.
    Cover and bake for 3 hours at 180°C (350°F). Remove lid 30 minutes before the end of cooking.
    Serves 8.

Blue vein steak

1 kg porterhouse steak
¾ C crumbled blue vein cheese
180 g butter, softened
1 tsp soy sauce
juice of half a lemon
1 clove garlic, crushed

Place all ingredients except steak in a food
processor and puree until smooth, or beat
vigorously together in a bowl. Meanwhile pan-fry
or grill steaks and pour sauce over when done.
Place under the griller to heat the sauce and serve
immediately.
  Serves 6.

New Zealand pie

A simplified domestic version of the meat pie, that great sustainer of the New Zealand workforce and travellers — especially railways passengers. Overseas visitors often go into ecstasy about these, which is surprising for many New Zealanders, who are either blase or scathing, especially about the commercial varieties. The secret of a really good pie is a generous filling: plenty of meat and a thin, crisp pastry.

Filling
450 g minced beef
2 onions, diced
2 t flour
½ t salt
½ t pepper
½ t sugar

Topping
1 heaped C flour
2 T fat or butter
2 t baking powder
pinch of salt
milk to mix

Place mince and onion in a saucepan with 1½ C water. Bring to the boil, then lower heat and add flour, salt, pepper and sugar mixed to a paste with a little water. Simmer for 1 hour. Transfer to a pie dish.

To prepare topping, rub fat or butter into flour and add baking powder and salt. Mix in enough milk to make a sticky dough, roll out and place on top of meat.

Bake at 250°C (475°F) for 15 minutes or until pastry is lightly browned. Traditionalists would insist on serving this with lashings of tomato sauce!

Serves 4–6.

Variation: To make individual pies as served in a New Zealand Railways cafetaria, prepare the filling only and use short pastry rolled out to line small pie dishes. Allow enough pastry for the lids.

Whiritoa ham steaks

4 ham steaks
1½ T brown sugar
1 t prepared hot mustard

Place steaks under the grill and cook for 5–8 minutes on one side only. Remove from heat, turn over and spread with mustard. Sprinkle with brown sugar. Reduce heat to avoid scorching the sugar and return to the grill for a further 5 minutes.
Serves 4.

Tamarillo pork chops

Here we have a homegrown modern dish which is rapidly approaching classic status because it is the ideal combination of a sweetish meat and a sharp fruit. It first appeared some time in the 1960s, perhaps from the sub-tropical fruit-growing area near Kerikeri, since the dish sometimes goes under the name of 'Kerikeri casserole'. The great athlete Peter Snell once voted it his favourite dish, thus ensuring it an everlasting place in Kiwi culture.

4 pork chops
4 tamarillos, peeled and sliced
2 small onions, sliced
1 medium apple, peeled and sliced
½ t salt
1 T brown sugar

Trim chops of excess fat and brown both sides in a pan. Place tamarillos, onions and apple in a saucepan and cook in 1 T water until soft. Place the browned chops in a casserole dish, sprinkle with salt and pour tamarillos, onions and apple over the top. Cover and bake at 160°C (325°F) for about 1 hour.
Serves 4.

Bacon and egg pie

Sadly, the bacon and egg pie so dear to the hearts of Kiwis is not a New Zealand invention at all, but has its origins in eighteenth-century England. However, we may take solace in the fact that ours is an adaptation; whereas the original recipe called for the eggs to be beaten, New Zealanders usually break in the eggs whole or slightly prick the yolks. Bacon and egg pie can be eaten hot, but as a cold picnic dish it stands unrivalled.

170 g shortcrust pastry (see recipe below)
3–4 rashers rindless bacon, halved
1 small onion, grated (optional)
4–5 eggs
milk or beaten egg for glazing

Cut pastry into two pieces, one slightly larger than the other. Roll out larger piece to cover the bottom of a pie dish. Line with halved bacon rashers. Break in eggs and either leave them whole or prick the yolks with a sharp knife. Add grated onion, if desired. Cover with remaining pastry and brush with milk or beaten egg. Bake for 15 minutes at 200°C (400°F), then reduce heat to 180°C (350°F) and cook for a further 30 minutes.

Short pastry
225 g flour
pinch salt
60 g butter
60 g lard

Sift flour and salt into a bowl. Rub the butter and lard into the flour with the tips of the fingers, or cut it in with a pastry blender or two knives held together. It is properly mixed when it looks like fresh breadcrumbs. Gradually sprinkle over a little cold water — just enough to hold the dough together and leave the sides of the mixing bowl clean. Knead lightly for a few seconds, then chill for 5 minutes before using. Store excess in freezer.
Serves 4.

Muttonbird

A muttonbird is the young of the sooty shearwater or titi, a type of seabird. The fact that it is very greasy may account for the name of muttonbird, for there ends any resemblance to sheepmeat. It is something of an acquired taste, with a flavour more akin to a mixture of wild duck and fish. The early Maori would trap the birds either during their migration periods by erecting nets on coastal cliffs and each evening building fires behind the nets to attract them to the light; or (as is more usual today) by taking the young, plump chicks from their burrows.

Muttonbird and potato pie

1 muttonbird
500 g cooked mashed potatoes
1 T butter
½ C milk
1 t chopped parsley
1 T butter
1 T flour
1 C milk

Boil muttonbird in three changes of cold water, for a total of 30 minutes. Bone and chop bird finely. Mix half the butter and milk with mashed potatoes and line a greased pie dish with it, reserving some for the top. Melt second measure of butter, blend in flour, add second measure of milk and bring to the boil to thicken, stirring continuously. Add muttonbird and parsley and pour over potato. Cover the top with remaining potato and score the top with a wet spoon. Bake in a hot oven until well browned.
Serves 4.

Muttonbird croquettes

120 g muttonbird
3 medium potatoes, boiled and mashed
flour
1 egg, beaten
breadcrumbs
oil or fat for frying

Boil muttonbird in 3 changes of water. Bone and chop flesh finely. Mix with mashed potatoes and roll into cylindrical shapes on a floured board. Dip in beaten egg, then roll in breadcrumbs. Fry in deep fat or oil until golden brown.
Serves 4.

Muttonbird paste

1 muttonbird
1 t anchovy essence

Boil the muttonbird in three changes of water. Pick the flesh from the bones and reduce to a paste in a food processor, or pass 3–4 times through a mincer. Mix in anchovy essence; no further seasoning is needed. Press into a small jar and refrigerate.
Spread on slices of wholemeal bread or use in sandwiches.

Pukeko

It seems a pity to shoot the pukeko, one of New Zealand's most colourful native birds, with its brilliant blue plumage and a distinctive red beak. Nevertheless, it is legal to do so during the open season. For best results, use a young, skinned bird; do not pluck. The legs are very sinewy and some cooks discard them altogether, using only the breast meat. The flesh is strongly flavoured.

Pukeko casserole

1 pukeko
5 rashers bacon
1 medium onion, diced
½ t thyme
salt and pepper
cornflour
juice and rind of half a lemon

Cut bird into bite-sized pieces. Line a casserole dish with bacon and place pukeko on top. Add onion, thyme, salt and pepper. Pour over 600 ml water. Cover and bake at 140°C (275°F) for 2 hours or until bird is tender. Remove meat, thicken gravy with cornflour mixed to a paste with a little water, and add lemon juice and rind.
    Serves 3.

Quail

Introduced near Auckland in 1862, Californian quail are widely distributed throughout the country, except in areas of native bush. They may be hunted in some areas during the open season. Whether quail need to be hung at all is a matter of controversy, but certainly they need no more than 2 days. Pluck the bird and cut off the head. Pull the skin down towards the body, cut off the neck as close as possible to the body, and remove entrails in preparation for stuffing. Allow at least one bird per serving.

Bluff quail

4 quail
8 oysters, chopped
1½ C fresh breadcrumbs
1 egg, beaten
1 T chopped parsley
salt and pepper
4 rashers bacon

Combine oysters, breadcrumbs, parsley and egg. Season to taste. Stuff each quail with this mixture and wrap each bird in a rasher of bacon. Roast at 180°C (350°F) for 25–30 minutes, and serve with crabapple jelly.
  Serves 4.

45

Wild duck

Each May some 50,000 duckshooters take to the swamplands and estuaries of New Zealand for the annual season. Four species of duck are legal game in season: mallard, grey, shoveller and paradise duck. Mallards, which were introduced from Britain in 1867, make up at least half the New Zealand duck population. As a table bird, the mallard is without peer: large and succulent, the drakes weighing about 1.5 kg and the female about 1.25 kg.

Birds should be plucked as soon as possible after shooting. To prepare them for plucking, immerse for a minute or two in near-boiling water to which washing soda has been added. This cuts through the oily waterproofing of the feathers and allows the hot water to reach the base of the quills. Pluck against the fall of the feathers, using thumb and forefingers. Cut out the oil sac at the base of the tail. Cut off the neck, but leave on the neck skin. Rinse and dry, then hang for 2–3 days.

Bake the birds at 150°C (300°F) for at least 3 hours: you can never be sure of a duck's age and long, slow cooking will ensure tenderness.

Whakamaru wild duck

2 wild duck
3 C fresh breadcrumbs
½ t mixed herbs
¾ C stewed apple
1 T butter
flour
milk
2 oranges, peeled and sliced
4 rashers bacon
dry sherry

Stuff ducks with a mixture of breadcrumbs, herbs, apple, butter and salt and pepper to taste. Truss and roll in flour. Place in an ovenproof dish and pour in equal quantities of milk and water to a level about half-way up the birds. Cover with orange slices and top with bacon rashers. Seal tightly with a lid, spreading a flour and water paste around the rim if necessary. Bake at 150°C (300°F) for at least 3 hours. Remove birds, mash orange into the pan juices and thicken with cornflour mixed to a paste with a little water. Add dry sherry to taste and serve sauce separately.
Serves 4.

Grilled wild duck

1 small wild duck, approx 700 g
60 g butter, melted
1 t salt
2 T hot water
¼ C red currant jelly, melted

Cut duck in half, rinse and wipe dry. Place skin-side down on a wire rack in a baking dish. Grill about 15 cm from the heat, brushing occasionally with a mixture of melted butter, salt and hot water. Turn after 10–15 minutes and grill other side for a similar time. Brush with melted red currant jelly and serve.
Serves 2.

Wild duck Canterbury style

2 ducks, jointed
butter
1 onion, sliced
45 g flour
2 C stock or water
1 whole onion
5 cloves
bunch mixed herbs
1⅓ cups port
2–3 turnips, boiled

Fry jointed ducks with onion in a little butter until golden brown. Remove duck, blend in flour, then stir in stock or water. Add whole onion stuck with cloves, herbs and port.

Replace duck and simmer gently for 1 hour. When tender remove and skim grease from sauce. Thicken with a cornflour paste if necessary and pour over duck. Garnish with pieces of fancy-cut turnip.
Serves 4.

Pheasant with apple

1 pheasant
50 g butter
4 eating apples, peeled and sliced
salt and pepper
½ C cream

Melt the butter in a heavy pot and brown the pheasant on all sides. Roast in a 180°C oven, allowing about half an hour for a medium-sized bird. Meanwhile, saute the slices of apple remaining in the pot until lightly browned. Add the pheasant and pack the apple slices around it. Pour over the cream, season well with salt and pepper, cover the pot and cook for 15 minutes at 180°C (350°F).

Serves 2.

Chicken

Not so very long ago, chicken was regarded as a special-occasion meat in New Zealand, reserved for Christmas and birthdays. Its high cost virtually banished it from everyday fare. Very few birds were bred especially for the table; those available in the shops were mostly 'boilers' — tough old birds raised as layers, whose laying days were over.

As recently as 1965, the per capita consumption of chicken was only 225 g a year. Then, large-scale chicken farms became established, buying patterns changed rapidly and consumption has increased more than 40-fold. More than half comes from fast-food outlets as part of the usual weekly fare.

Chicken with sultana stuffing

The dried fruit stuffing used here reflects the traditionally festive role of chicken in New Zealand's national cuisine.

1 large chicken
1 C cooked rice
75 g sultanas
12–15 roasted almonds, chopped roughly
1 T chopped parsley
1 small onion, finely diced
¼ t oregano
2 t butter, melted

Mix rice with sultanas, almonds, parsley, onion and oregano.
Season to taste and pour over melted butter. Fill chicken cavity lightly and sew up. Rub the outside skin with a little butter and sprinkle lightly with salt and pepper.

Place in a roasting pan with a little water and cook at 180°C (350°F), allowing 55 minutes per kg of stuffed weight, plus an extra 20 minutes. Baste during cooking. For the last 10–12 minutes, turn the temperature up to 200°C (400°F) to crisp the skin. The chicken can be tested for doneness by poking a skewer between the thigh and body of the chicken. If a pinkish liquid oozes out, the chicken needs more cooking: if it comes out clear, the chicken is done.

If using an oven bag to roast the chicken, allow 40 minutes per kg and remove from bag 10 minutes before serving.
Serves 4.

Chicken Whakatane

An elusive and decidedly unevocative title for a delicious dish which is actually a cross between crumbed chicken and coq au vin.

1 medium chicken
½ C flour
¼ t mace
60 g butter
1 C sliced spring onions
1 medium onion, sliced
4 cloves garlic, crushed
½ C white wine
450 g tomatoes, peeled and chopped
2 green peppers, sliced

Joint chicken into 4 pieces and wipe dry. Place in a plastic bag with flour, salt, pepper and mace. Shake until pieces are well covered. Fry gently in butter until lightly browned, remove from pan and keep warm.

In the same pan, saute spring onions, garlic and onions until cooked but not brown. Place in a casserole dish and cover with chicken pieces. Pour over wine.

Bake at 160°C (325°F) for 40 minutes. Add tomatoes and green peppers 10 minutes before the end of cooking.
Serves 4.

Chicken with stuffing crust

1 large chicken, cut into pieces
2 T butter
2 T flour
½ C milk
2 C soft breadcrumbs
2 T melted butter
1 medium onion, finely diced
½ t sage
½ t thyme
salt and pepper
3 rashers rindless bacon, diced

Barely cover chicken pieces with water and boil for 20 minutes until just tender. Remove chicken and reserve liquor. Melt first measure of butter in a pan and blend in flour. Add milk and 1½ C chicken liquor and bring to the boil to thicken, stirring continuously.

Place chicken pieces in a casserole dish and pour over sauce. Toss breadcrumbs in second measure of butter and mix in onion, sage and thyme. Season to taste with salt and pepper. Sprinkle mixture over chicken and top with pieces of bacon. Bake at 180°C (350°F) for 1 hour.
Serves 4–6.

Coconut Chicken

A specialty of the Samoans, who form the largest group of Pacific Islanders living in New Zealand.

Ardent traditionalists may want to make their own coconut cream by grating 2–3 fresh ripe coconuts and squeezing the flesh through muslin. A second extraction may then be made by mixing 1 C water or milk with the flesh and squeezing again. Coconut cream can also be made by scalding 1 C milk with 1 C desiccated coconut, soaking for 30 minutes, then squeezing through muslin. But it is a laborious task; the cans of ready-made coconut cream are quite acceptable.

This recipe owes its origin in part to the classic Samoan dish palusami, which is made by baking young taro leaves and coconut cream, usually flavoured with onion and salt, and wrapped in banana leaves, in the umu (hot stones oven).

1 kg chicken, boned and cut into 2 cm cubes
1½ T shortening or oil
1½ t salt
450 g spinach
2 T butter
½ t salt
1 C coconut cream

Brown cubes of chicken for several minutes in hot shortening or oil and the first measure of salt. Pour over ½ C water, cover tightly and simmer for 10 minutes. Drain well.

Meanwhile, wash spinach and place it, dripping wet, in a saucepan with melted butter and second measure of salt. Cover tightly and simmer for 10–15 minutes and drain well. Add to drained chicken in pot and pour over coconut cream. Bring to the boil over a low heat, stirring occasionally. Serve with boiled taro or kumara.
Serves 4–6.

Venison

The status of deer is somewhat of an enigma: they were introduced as a game animal by one generation, despised as the agent of erosion by the next, and prized as a lucrative export by yet another.

The red deer, introduced in 1861, is the most widespread species. Others include the fallow deer of Europe, wapiti and whitetail deer of North America, rusa and sambar deer from southeast Asia, and the sika deer of Japan. Good quality venison is dark red, finely grained and has firm white fat. Sika and fallow venison is regarded as the best, but age and condition of the animal are important considerations as well. All venison should be hung for 2 days to more than a week before eating, depending on the animal's age.

Medallions of venison Franz Josef

One of the early introductions of deer was a gift from the Emperor Franz Josef of Austria; a famous glacier in the Southern Alps also bears his name. This recipe comes from Auckland's Top of the Town restaurant, which has won a number of awards, including the Diners' Club Restaurant of the Year in 1989 and 1990.

4 x 115 g venison medallions, cut from saddle
1 t salt
1 t pepper
pinch thyme
45 g butter
2 shallots, sliced into rings
120 g mushrooms, sliced
4 juniper berries (optional)
¼ C brandy
300 ml cream
2 poached pears, halved
4 t red currant jelly

Flatten medallions with a heavy object. Rub with salt, pepper and thyme and fry in butter. In a separate pan fry the shallots, then add mushrooms and juniper berries. Pour the brandy over and set alight. Add cream and stir on a low heat until sauce thickens. Pour sauce over cooked medallions and top each with a half pear filled with red currant jelly.
Serves 4.

Kumara-topped stuffed venison

1 kg venison, cut into thin strips
1 onion, finely diced
½ t chopped parsley
½ t sage
1 t salt
pinch pepper
2 C fresh breadcrumbs
60 g butter, melted
2 C cooked mashed kumara
¾ C grated tasty cheese

Make a stuffing by combining onion, parsley, sage, salt, pepper and breadcrumbs. Mix in melted butter.

Place a layer of venison in the bottom of a greased casserole. Cover with a layer of stuffing. Repeat layers of venison and stuffing, finishing with a layer of venison. Cover and bake at 180°C (350°F), for 1–1½ hrs.

Remove from oven and spread over a layer of mashed kumara. Top with grated cheese and bake uncovered in a hot oven until cheese is lightly browned.
Serves 6.

Waioika venison

1.5 kg venison steak, cubed
¼ C flour
1 large onion, sliced
2 rashers bacon, diced
3 T oil
1 t salt
½ t pepper
3 cloves
¼ t nutmeg
1 T brown sugar
½ C red wine

Roll venison cubes in flour. Fry with onion and bacon in oil until slightly browned. Remove and place in an ovenproof dish with salt, pepper, cloves, nutmeg, sugar and wine. Add water just to cover.

Bake at 160°C (325°F) for 2½ hours. If necessary, thicken with cornflour paste before serving.
Serves 8.

Rabbit

Rabbits were introduced between 1840 and 1864, ironically with the intention of starting a trade in meat and skins, but in fact they have almost bankrupted many farmers by their relentless breeding and grazing. Local rabbit meat has been banned from sale since 1954, but imported meat is still legal. This has led to the ludicrous situation where rabbit meat is imported from China — when our paddocks are teeming with them.

Rabbit and prune casserole

1 rabbit, jointed
450 ml red wine
2 T white vinegar
6 peppercorns
2 bay leaves
½ t thyme
small sprig rosemary
120 g prunes, pitted
60 g butter
45 g flour
salt and pepper

Marinate rabbit overnight in wine, vinegar, peppercorns, bay leaves, thyme, rosemary and prunes. Wipe joints dry and lightly brown in butter. Transfer to a casserole dish and blend flour into remaining butter in a pan. Strain wine mixture (put prunes into casserole and discard herbs) and add slowly to flour and butter, stirring over a low heat until sauce thickens. Season to taste. Pour sauce over rabbit and prunes, cover casserole dish and bake for 2 hours at 140°C (275°F).
Serves 2–3.

Hare

The first hares reached New Zealand shores after jumping overboard from a ship in Lyttelton Harbour. But despite this determined beginning, they have never bred on the same scale as rabbits. While rabbit may be compared to chicken in flavour and texture, hare has a much more distinctively gamey flavour and coarser texture.

Jugged hare

This is, of course, a traditional English dish, but is so popular in New Zealand that I have included it here.

1 kg hare portions
60 g butter, preferably clarified
900 ml beef stock
¾ C port wine or claret
1 medium onion
6 cloves
juice and grated rind of 1 lemon
2 bay leaves
½ t thyme
½ t rosemary
½ t allspice
30 g flour
30 g butter

Brown hare portions in hot butter, remove and place in an earthenware casserole along with onion stuck with cloves. Cover with stock, wine, lemon juice and rind. Add bay leaves, thyme, rosemary and allspice tied together in a muslin bag. Cover and bake at 180°C (350°F) for 2–3 hours or until tender. About 30 minutes before serving, knead together flour and the second measure of butter, place in a cup and blend in a little of the casserole juice. Add to casserole to thicken.
Serves 3–4.

Opossum

A national dish? Many New Zealanders are horrified at the thought of eating a noxious animal, better known for its devastating effects on the native bush than for its culinary qualities. Nevertheless, the opossum is a clean eater, so there can be no objection to the quality of the meat. It is, however, rather strongly flavoured, so some people prefer to boil it and discard the water before using it. Young females are said to be more mildly flavoured and tender than older or male animals; at best, the flavour is likened to chicken.

It is essential to remove the two whitish glands near the base of the tail, which will taint the meat. To be sure of removing them completely, cut out the backbone to about 13 cm up from the tail.

Opossum bacon bake

1.5 kg opossum meat
6 T flour
1 t salt
¼ t pepper
60 g butter
4 rashers bacon
2 medium onions, sliced
600 ml mutton or beef stock
2 T port or sherry
120 g carrots, sliced
1 sprig parsley
2 bay leaves
¼ t marjoram
¼ t thyme
2 T cream or top milk
cornflour

Cut opossum into joints, rinse and wipe dry. Roll joints in flour seasoned with salt and pepper, then brown lightly in butter on both sides. Transfer to a casserole dish lined with bacon rashers. Saute onions in butter and place over opossum pieces in casserole.

Blend surplus flour into remaining butter in pan. Stir in stock and bring to the boil, stirring continuously. Add to casserole together with port and sherry or carrots. Tie up parsley, bay leaves, marjoram and thyme in a muslin bag and add to casserole. Bake at 180°C (350°F) for 3 hours, or until meat comes away from the bones. Remove herbs, add cream and thicken with cornflour if necessary.

Serves 5-6.

Vegetables and Salads

One of New Zealand's less fortunate legacies from Mother England's cookery was a tendency to treat vegetables merely as a plain, boiled adjunct to the roast, rather than as a feature in themselves. The fact that, historically, New Zealanders could afford to eat meat with almost every meal, compounded this habit.

Since the dawn of the organic age in the 1970s, however, the reign of 'meat and three veg' has come increasingly under siege. While strict vegetarians remain a small minority, their influence has been felt as red meat consumption drops and the range of exotic new green vegetables on the market grows ever greater. To the modern New Zealand cook, the idea of an all-vegetable meal is no longer the heresy it once was.

Kumara or sweet potato

A wealth of varied and conflicting legend surrounds the arrival of the kumara in New Zealand. Several traditions speak of canoe voyages back to the former homeland of Hawaiki to obtain kumaras for planting, but some if not all of these may refer to internal migrations within New Zealand. Groups who ventured too far south in their exploration of the islands must sometimes have lost their crops from unexpected frosts in late spring or early autumn, and been forced to send messengers back as far as Northland or the Bay of Plenty to get more.

There is now little doubt that the primary migration to New Zealand in the seventh or eighth centuries brought to the Maori food plants from an eastern Polynesian homeland, probably in the Society or Marquesas islands. The kumara proved to be the most successful because it matured in the shortest time and thrived in the light sandy soils which the Maori were able to work with digging sticks. Consequently it became the most valuable cultivated food to the pre-European Maori.

The early Maori settlers spread rapidly through New Zealand and tried to grow kumaras as far south as Nelson and North Canterbury. Erosion became a problem in some areas as coastal and lowland forest was burned off to make new gardens. There is also evidence that the climatic change around the beginning of the seventeenth century tipped the balance against successful kumara-growing in these marginal areas. Some Maori groups were forced to give up gardening altogether and to gather fernroot as their main source of starch.

Cultivation techniques were quite sophisticated. In the Rotorua-Taupo area tubers may have been pre-sprouted in starter beds and later transplanted, but generally the small tubers were planted directly in low mounds in late spring. Gravelly subsoil, sand and wood ash were often scattered over the ground, and brush fences were erected to shelter the plants from wind. In cooler climates baskets were placed over the plants at night to protect them from frost. Smouldering branches of kawakawa (pepper tree) kept insects at bay. However, the traditional Maori kumara became rapidly supplanted with the introduction in the 1850s of the American varieties of sweet potato, and almost all kumaras grown today are varieties developed from these. Only recent efforts have saved the traditional kumara varieties from extinction.

The kumara is an amazingly versatile vegetable which goes especially well with sweetish meats such as pork or chicken, and also can be cooked with just about any fruit. However, the best way to bring out the full, sweet flavour of kumaras is to bake or roast them in the oven.

Cooking kumaras

Baked. Scrub kumaras but do not peel. Cut large ones in half crossways. Place directly on to the oven rack and bake at 180°C (350°F) for 1 hour or more. If kumaras are to be sliced or cubed, they should be baked until barely tender. If, however, they are to be eaten in their jackets or mashed, then they should be baked until they feel soft when squeezed.

Roasted. Peel kumaras thinly and trim the thin tails. Place in a roasting dish with meat and turn in the fat. Cook for about 2 hours at 180°C (350°F). It is hard to overcook kumaras, but turn them occasionally to prevent drying out.

Boiled. Kumaras cook far more quickly this way, but much of the flavour disappears into the water. If you must boil them, never peel or cut them before cooking. Cook in a vegetable steamer if possible, and test with a skewer after about 20 minutes.

Kumara with meringue topping

Serve this with pork or chicken or as a vegetarian main dish.

2 C cooked mashed kumara
1 egg, separated
2 T butter
½ t salt
1 banana, sliced
¼ C castor sugar

Mix mashed kumara with egg yolk, butter and salt. Place in a greased casserole dish and arrange banana slices over the top. Bake 30 minutes at 180°C (350°F).

Beat sugar and egg white stiffly and spread over the top 10 minutes before the end of cooking.
Serves 4.

Spiced kumaras

1 kg kumaras
whole cloves
¼ C brown sugar
1 t ground cinnamon
60 g butter

Bake or boil kumaras in their jackets until half cooked. Peel and stud each kumara with several cloves. Place in a greased ovenproof dish and sprinkle with a mixture of brown sugar and cinnamon.

Dot with small pieces of butter and bake for 30–40 minutes at 200°C (400°F).
Serves 4.

Kumara and banana souffle

Either serve this as a stylish accompaniment to the meat course, or as the main dish of a vegetarian meal.

4 medium kumaras
2 small bananas, mashed
2 eggs, separated
¼ C milk
¼ t ground nutmeg
salt

Bake or boil kumaras in their jackets. Peel and mash. Add bananas, egg yolks, milk, nutmeg and salt to taste, and beat together well. Fold in stiffly beaten egg white.

Transfer mixture to a buttered oven dish and bake at 200°C (400°F) for 25 minutes.
Serves 4.

Kumara and orange cups

1 kg kumaras
2 T cream or top milk
½ t salt
3 oranges
1 T brown sugar
1 C grated tasty cheese

Bake or boil kumaras in their jackets, peel and mash with cream and salt. Cut oranges in half and scoop out flesh, leaving skin intact. Remove pith and chop oranges finely. Sprinkle with brown sugar and mix with kumara.

Pile into orange halves, sprinkle with cheese and reheat at 180°C (350°F) for 15 minutes or until cheese is melted.
Serves 4–6.

Green vegetables

New Zealand is not well endowed with native green vegetables. In fact, apart from puha the only native green in common use today is New Zealand spinach, the celebrated antiscorbutic (preventer of scurvy) which James Cook's botanist, Sir Joseph Banks, discovered in Queen Charlotte Sound and took back to Britain in 1770. By the nineteenth century it had spread to Europe and the United States, and nowadays it is also grown in China, Japan, Chile and all over the Pacific.

New Zealand spinach still grows wild but it is more commonly cultivated today. It has succulent, triangular leaves and trails over the ground, thriving in sunny dry conditions. In most recipes it can safely be substituted for ordinary spinach.

As for New Zealand's introduced green vegetables, the most commonly eaten — peas, beans, cabbage, lettuce, Brussels sprouts, cauliflower, marrow, leeks and onions — together with root vegetables such as parsnips and carrots — are stolidly British in character.

There is, however, a difference in emphasis on some vegetables. Silverbeet (known in other countries as Swiss chard) is more popular in New Zealand than in Britain or elsewhere, perhaps only because it is so easy to grow here. (It is often used interchangeably with spinach.)

The same applies to pumpkin. While other people (notably the Americans) use it in soups and pies, New Zealanders seem to be alone in their practice of roasting pieces of pumpkin (often unskinned) with meat and other vegetables.

The post-war years have seen a gradual acceptance of more exotic vegetables into New Zealand cooking. Among the first of these were sweet corn, asparagus and green peppers (capsicums).

Whether as a result of the influence of Italian and Greek immigrants, the mass media, or the overseas travel boom, New Zealanders in the 1970s suddenly discovered broccoli, zucchini and eggplant (aubergine). Likewise, Chinese vegetables such as bean sprouts and Chinese cabbage (bok choy) began to take on, coupled with a growth of interest in ethnic cooking of all kinds.

Our sprawling 'quarter-acre' subdivisions have turned New Zealanders into a nation of home gardeners. From their backyards, countless suburban households can boast a year-round supply of garden-fresh vegetables — even if as a nation we have been so often accused of not knowing how to cook them. However true this may have been in the past, New Zealanders today are generally far more aware of how unappetising and devoid of nutrition overcooked green vegetables can be. The following recipes help to put paid to that 'boiled spud and cabbage' legend.

Broccoli with lemon butter

700 g broccoli
salt
115 g butter, melted
1½ T lemon juice
pepper

Trim broccoli of the coarser leaves and tough parts of stems. Cut into serving portions and sprinkle with salt. Steam or boil in salted water until tender. Stir together butter, lemon juice and pepper and pour over broccoli. Serve immediately.
Serves 4.

Curried cabbage

1 medium head cabbage, sliced
3 T butter
1 medium onion, grated
3 T flour
3 t curry powder
2 C milk
salt and pepper

Steam cabbage in salted water for 10 minutes. Meanwhile melt butter and fry onion until cooked. Blend in flour and curry powder, add milk and bring to the boil to thicken, stirring continuously. Mix in cooked cabbage and serve.
Serves 6.

Cabbage with caraway seeds and bacon

This is guaranteed to turn the most scorned vegetable in the world into the most praised dish of your dinner.

½ medium head cabbage, finely sliced
4 rashers bacon
1½ t caraway seeds, bruised

Grill the bacon on both sides and reserve the fat. Chop the bacon into pieces. Heat bacon fat in a large pan or wok, add the cabbage and caraway seeds, and stir fry the cabbage until cooked but still crisp. Add bacon pieces.
Serves 4.

Gingered carrots

450 g carrots
2 T butter
1 T grated fresh ginger root
2 t brown sugar
salt and pepper

Peel and slice carrots into sticks. Steam or boil in salted water until barely tender and drain. Add butter, ginger and brown sugar and fry quickly for several minutes. Season to taste with salt and pepper.
   Serves 4.

Mashed carrot and parsnip

500 g carrots, peeled and sliced
500 g parsnips, peeled and sliced
100 g butter
salt and pepper

Steam or boil the carrots and parsnips together until soft, then mash well, mixing in the butter and adding salt and pepper to taste.
   Serves 4–6.

Kamokamo

In view of the recent popularity of zucchini among sophisticated New Zealand cooks, it is ironic that a very similar vegetable has been quietly grown by Maori for the past 150 years, yet otherwise has been largely ignored.

   Introduced by Europeans, the kamokamo was readily accepted by the Maoris, who, it is thought, coined the name from 'cucumber'. It is, however, more accurately described as a form of squash and, like the zucchini, is best eaten when young and sweet. The nineteenth-century Maoris, however, also dried and then hollowed out the fully matured specimens for use as food and drink containers. In Canterbury these were used to store wine carefully produced from the juice of tutu berries (all other parts of the plant being deadly poisonous).

Kamokamo with cream and rosemary

2 T butter, preferably clarified
500 g kamokamo, diced
1 12-cm sprig fresh rosemary
salt and black pepper
4 T cream

In a large frying pan melt the butter and add the kamokamo, along with the sprig of rosemary which you have crushed in your fist to bring out the scent. Season with salt and pepper and fry about 5 minutes, stirring frequently.
   Add the cream and cook another 4–5 minutes. The kamokamo should still be slightly crunchy.
   Serves 3.

Red Cross tomatoes

This very patriotic dish, usually served as a light lunch, originated on the New Zealand home front during World War I.

4 large round tomatoes
4 eggs
4 T fat

Slice the bottoms off the tomatoes and reserve. Scoop sufficient pulp out of each tomato to receive an egg, then break in a whole egg. Melt fat and when boiling pour about ½ T over each egg to set it. Place tomatoes in remaining fat and cook from below. Slice tomato bottoms into cross shapes and place over the eggs when cooked.
   Serves 4.

Salads

Salads have always been popular in New Zealand because of the temperate climate, but fondness does not necessarily imply expertise. The traditional New Zealand salad, indeed, was often a ghastly affair. Allow me to revive the memory: first, lettuce was cut into fine shreds, preferably using a blunt, serrated-edged knife so that the edges were nicely bruised. Then some eggs were boiled until the outsides of the yolks turned grey, cut into quarters and tossed into the bowl along with, perhaps, some soft tomatoes and overdeveloped radishes rescued from the bottom of the fridge. Then the dressing: two parts sweetened condensed milk to one of malt vinegar. Oh, and the decoration: a few slices of tinned beetroot about the top . . .

Of course the Great New Zealand Salad was never quite that bad, but times have changed and so have our tastes. Now that it is possible to buy good salad oils, interesting vinegars and a wider range of salad greens, the possibilities for exciting new salads grow ever larger. Nevertheless, even the most sophisticated Kiwis still enjoy the old-fashioned condensed-milk dressing now and again; the flavour of forgotten childhood food sparks a nostalgia even stronger than family snapshots or period pop songs.

Kapai salad

Very typical of the old school of New Zealand salad making this one, so no wonder it has been dubbed 'kapai' ('OK'). Using a sharp knife will minimise bruising, as will serving the salad as soon as possible after making.

1 lettuce, shredded
3 radishes, diced
2 spring onions, sliced
1 cucumber, peeled and sliced
2 hard-boiled eggs, diced
Dressing
2 T vinegar
¼ C cream
1½ T sugar

Combine shredded lettuce with radishes, onion, cucumber and hard-boiled eggs. Shake together vinegar, cream and sugar in a screw-top jar and pour over.
Serves 3–4.

New Zealand-style salad dressing

This classic New Zealand mayonnaise has stood the test of time.

1 × 400-g can sweetened condensed milk
about 300 ml vinegar
1 t salt
1 t pepper
1 t dry mustard

Empty condensed milk into a bowl. Three-quarters fill the empty can with vinegar, top up with water and add. Beat together with salt, pepper and mustard.

Apple and cream salad

A specialty of the Midland Hotel in Wellington, built in 1915 in the grand Spanish Mission style, but sadly demolished in 1982.

2 large fresh crisp red apples
juice of 1–2 lemons
2 t sugar
3 T raisins
150 ml cream

Cut apples into quarters, remove core, then slice each quarter lengthways again. Do not peel. Now slice crossways, and you should end up with small, neat wedges of apple.
Sprinkle lemon juice and sugar over the apple wedges and leave for 5 minutes or so to soak in. Pour over the raisins and cream and mix well.
Serves 4.

Kumara and banana salad

450 g kumaras
4 ripe bananas, sliced
¼ C lemon juice
¼ C sliced spring onions
½ C mayonnaise
1 clove garlic, crushed
2 t curry powder

Bake or boil kumaras in their skins. Peel and cut into cubes. Meanwhile marinate banana slices in lemon juice for 20–30 minutes. Combine banana, kumara and spring onions. Stir in mayonnaise mixed with garlic and curry powder.

Serves 6.

Kerikeri corn salad

1 × 450-g tin whole kernel sweet corn, drained
or 2 C cooked fresh sweet corn
1 C green peas, cooked
1 C diced cucumber
1 T chopped spring onion
2 t chopped chives
½ C diced green pepper
Dressing
1 clove garlic, crushed
¼ C salad oil
1 T vinegar

Combine corn, peas, cucumber, spring onion, chives and green pepper. Place garlic, oil, vinegar, salt and pepper in a screw-top jar, shake vigorously and pour over vegetables.

Serves 4–6.

Zucchini salad

700 g unpeeled zucchini, sliced
½ t salt
2 cloves garlic, crushed
oil and vinegar dressing
½ head lettuce
1 medium tomato, sliced
1 small green pepper, cut into rings
pinch paprika

Place zucchini in just enough boiling water to cover, add salt and garlic and boil for just 2–3 minutes. Drain, allow to cool, then refrigerate.

Toss zucchini in dressing, then place on a bed of torn lettuce leaves and decorate with tomato slices and green pepper rings. Sprinkle with paprika.

Serves 3–4.

Eggs and Cheese

Traditionally inexpensive and very versatile. New Zealand's dairy products provide the basis of many lunch dishes and are, of course, an important source of protein for vegetarians.

The origins of dairying in New Zealand stretch right back to the first Christian missionary, Samuel Marsden, who first introduced cattle to the country in 1814. However, until the main European settlements became established, milking-cows were very rare and confined mainly to coastal areas; an early Nelson settler, W.T. Pratt, records that in the earliest days of Nelson settlement a cow cost 50 pounds. As dairy herds (imported mainly from New South Wales) increased, excess produce was bartered with storekeepers for other household necessities. There was no cooling or other special treatment of milk, but spoilage was not a problem while it was being sold only locally.

Distance prohibited overseas trade in dairy perishables until the great boon of refrigerated cargoes, from which New Zealand continues to benefit today.

Eggs

New Zealanders eat a great quantity of eggs — an average of 288 a year each in fact. This puts us in the top league of egg-consuming nations, along with Israel and the United States.

To boil an egg is supposedly the simplest culinary operation there is, but even this skill is the subject of controversy among connoisseurs. There is an incident on record where the chef of a university hostel was watching a newly hired cook boil some eggs.

'Wait until the water boils before you put them in,' he said. The new cook politely but firmly disagreed. His way was to start with cold water. Both stuck obstinately to their positions, until the chef added weight to his argument with a playful slap to the cook's face, then fists began flying. (On this boiling issue might I suggest a diplomatic solution: have the water just faintly bubbling before lowering the egg in gently with a spoon, then turn the heat up full.)

Another vexed question is the cooking time. A 3-minute egg will still be very runny, while 4 minutes will just set the white but leave the yolk runny. The yolk of a 4½-minute egg will be just soft but not runny. Allow 10 minutes for a hard-boiled egg and peel it as soon as it is cooked. Always start with the egg at room temperature — it is more likely to crack if taken straight from the refrigerator.

Omelettes

If only making an omelette could be as scientific as boiling an egg! An omelette should never take long to make, but exactly how long depends on how quickly the bottom cooks in relation to the top. The heat and thus the time must be adjusted accordingly. A good emergency measure if your souffle omelette is not setting on top, is to put it under the griller.

Often ignored, but very suitable for flavouring omelettes and souffles, are New Zealand's many varieties of seafood. In fact, in terms of flavour relative to the amount used, seafoods are the best omelette and souffle flavourings of all. The airy texture of both souffle and omelette is the perfect medium for the subtle seafood flavour.

Souffle omelette

This is an uncomplicated and absolutely fail-safe way of producing a deliciously puffy omelette, as taught to me by Eelco Boswijk of the Chez Eelco restaurant in Nelson.

3 eggs
¼ t salt
black pepper
knob of butter

Break eggs into a smallish bowl. Add salt and a little ground black pepper, then run in about ½ T cold water from the tap. Beat with a hand beater as fast as you possibly can, until the eggs have fluffed up considerably.

Heat butter in a heavy-bottomed frying pan until sizzling vigorously but not burning, then pour in eggs all at once. (If the heat is right, the eggs should hiss; if they don't, the pan is too cool.) Cook over a medium/high heat for 3–4 minutes. When a spongy crust has formed on the bottom, lift up one corner with a spatula to check that it is not browning too quickly compared with the top. Reduce heat if necessary, but remember that there will be a thin layer of uncooked egg on the top at the end of cooking.

If using a filling, place over one side of the omelette just as it begins to set. Fold over the other side and serve at once.

Curried eggs

4 hard-boiled eggs, quartered
1 small onion, grated
1 small apple, grated
2 T butter
2 T flour
1 t curry powder
1 C milk
salt and pepper

Fry onion and apple in butter until cooked but not browned. Mix in flour and curry powder and cook for 1–2 minutes. Add milk and bring to the boil to thicken, stirring continuously. Season to taste and cook for several minutes. Add eggs and heat through.
Serves 4.

Cheese

In the 1980s, New Zealand cheese suddenly came of age. The number of varieties produced leapt from 16 to 60, largely as a result of a new phenomenon, the small-scale craft cheesemaker. Ancient techniques of smearing, ageing and rinding were revived and combined with the best of twentieth-century technology, totally revitalising the industry. Finally, in 1989 New Zealand surprised the world when a raclette cheese made by Ferndale Dairies in Eltham gained second place in the open class of the European Cheese Championship, competing against 41 cheeses of all types and from all the big cheesemaking countries of the world.

Ferndale raclette outscored all other raclettes and failed by only one point to win the top award, receiving a total of 91 points out of a possible 100. Of the three other European raclettes entered, none scored higher than 80 points. If these results are any indication, then the best raclette in the world is not made in the Swiss Alps but right here in New Zealand.

While cheesemaking had been practised as a cottage industry in the very early days of European settlement of New Zealand, it was not until 1871 that a co-operative of dairy farmers on the Otago Peninsula established the country's first commercial cheese factory.

Cheddar was the first and for many years the only variety to be produced in New Zealand. It had of course been popular in the Old Country and was the first to be adapted to a standard method of production. Most importantly, cheddar is one of the few cheeses which actually improve with the time it takes a cargo ship to reach the other side of the world, and it was the type of cheese John Bull wanted to buy right up until our cosy trading relationship was shattered by Britain's entry into the EEC.

Since that time, the vast majority of New Zealand export cheese (at least 70 percent) has ended up in the melting vats of Japanese, American or European processed-cheese factories, a situation forced upon us by the protectionist policies of our client countries: in Europe we cannot sell table cheese of any kind, while in the United States rigid limits on the types and quantities of what we can export leave no room for diversification.

Some famous New Zealand cheese varieties

Cheddar. In the eyes of the rest of the world, cheddar probably still is *the* New Zealand cheese. Until the 1960s, it was made in hundreds of tiny, labour-intensive factories scattered all over the country's dairying regions. However, modern technology has paved the way for today's giant, fully automated cheddar factories. Buyers are now offered 17 major specifications, for example with higher fat or protein content.

Cheddar is the ultimate cooking cheese. Not only is it relatively cheap, but it melts well and retains its flavour with heating.

Egmont. This was New Zealand's first original cheese type, developed in the early 1960s to meet the demands of an emerging Japanese market for a mild gouda-style cheese. The name was coined in honour of the Fuji-shaped mountain in the heart of New Zealand's dairy country. Egmont can be cooked but its subtle, sweetish flavour is dissipated somewhat with heating, and it is probably more suited to the cheeseboard or to add textural interest to salads.

Blue Vein. As a nation descended from stilton-loving immigrants, New Zealand has inherited a strong British tradition of blue cheese. Blue Vein, perfected in 1951 after extensive trials, is now exported to more than 25 countries and has

become recognised internationally as a variety in its own right. It can be distinguished from its European counterparts by the deeper yellow colour of its curd. This arises from a difference in milk colour. The whiter European milk is taken from cows which are kept in barns during the winter and fed with grains and supplements, while New Zealand's more equable climate allows cows to be fed on grass all year round.

As part of the manufacturing process, the cheeses are pierced with stainless steel needles. Spores are then allowed to enter the holes and develop the mould. Blue Vein's soft, crumbly texture makes it blend well for sauces, dressing, or dips, and it is also excellent in salads.

In recent years several exciting new blue cheeses have been developed by Ferndale Dairies of Eltham: a richer version of Blue Vein known as Blue Supreme, another known as Bleu de Montagne, and a delicious cross between a Camembert and a blue cheese, known as Bleu de Bresse. These are all much too expensive to contemplate for any other use than the cheeseboard.

Another recent development is Hipikaha (Maori for 'strong sheep'), a sheep's milk blue cheese developed by Ross McCallum of Kapiti Cheeses near Wellington. This is superbly rich and sweet, and probably the nearest thing to a classic roquefort we have yet seen in this country.

Farmhouse. Otherwise known as Whitestone, after the factory in Oamaru which produces it exclusively, this is the brainchild of Colin Dennison, a craft cheesemaker of Waikouaiti near Dunedin. It is a gouda-style white curd cheese subjected to high-humidity curing, with a camembert mould on the outside. It is far too special to be used in cooking, and needs only a lively, full-bodied Cabernet Sauvignon to accompany it.

Aorangi. Another brie or camembert style cheese, this was discovered by accident when Kapiti cheesemaker Ross McCallum set out to make a brie. It did not turn out as intended, but the customer liked it, and the result is a great white wedding cake of a cheese, slightly more acidic than conventional brie, with a delicious mushroom-like edge to the flavour. Another cheeseboard cheese.

Riverlea Red. Riverlea is a small village near Eltham in Taranaki, where this original New Zealand variety was developed by the New Zealand Co-operative Rennet Co. A semi-firm, sweet curd, brine-salted cheese, it is mild and clean in flavour. It is an attractive addition to any cheeseboard, but can also be used for cooking.

Lunch dishes using cheese

Most New Zealanders consider cheese too rich to eat for breakfast and reserve their evening main course for meat, poultry or fish. Midday, then, is the ideal time to serve a cheese dish.

Cheese, kumara and bacon pie

Long before Quiche Lorraine was thrashed to death in the 1970s and 80s, Kiwi jokers were eating cheese pie without a second thought. This is a complete lunch in itself.

2 medium kumara, peeled and sliced
salt and pepper
3 rashers rindless bacon, halved
1½ t prepared hot mustard
1 medium cooking apple, peeled and sliced
2 medium onions, cut into rings
1½ C grated tasty cheddar cheese

Arrange kumara slices in the bottom of a greased ovenproof dish and sprinkle lightly with salt and pepper. Spread bacon with mustard, place half the quantity over the kumara, cover with sliced apple, then top with remaining bacon and mustard. Cover with onion rings and sprinkle lightly with salt and pepper. Finish with a layer of grated cheese and pour ¼ C hot water down the side of the dish. Cover with a lid and bake for 1½ hours at 180°C (350°F).
    Serves 3–4.

Cheese, tomatoes and corn casserole

½ C grated cheddar or Egmont cheese
6 small tomatoes, sliced
2 C corn kernels, fresh or tinned
1 t sugar
pinch pepper
½ t salt
1 C dry breadcrumbs
2 T butter, melted

Mix together grated cheese, tomatoes and corn. Sprinkle with sugar, salt and pepper and placed in a greased ovenproof dish. Toss breadcrumbs in melted butter and sprinkle over the top. Bake for 20 minutes at 180°C (350°F).
    Serves 4.

Dinner dishes using cheese

Vegetarians might justifiably complain that traditional New Zealand cooking has little to offer them — except, of course, for the basic ingredients with which to experiment themselves. To ameliorate that state of affairs, here are three meatless main-course dishes, typically Kiwi in their solidity, and which 'carnivores' may also enjoy for a change. These should be accompanied by lighter green vegetables or salads.

Cheese pudding

600 ml milk
30 g butter
125 g fresh breadcrumbs
90 g tasty cheddar, grated
2 eggs, beaten

Heat milk and butter together until just boiling, then pour over breadcrumbs. Whisk to a smooth consistency, then add grated cheese. Season to taste with salt and pepper and stir in beaten eggs. Transfer mixture to a buttered oven dish and bake for 30–35 minutes at 180°C (350°F).
    Serves 3–4.

Egg, cheese and corn savoury

2 eggs, beaten
¾ C milk
½ T butter, melted
115 g fresh breadcrumbs
1 x 310-g can cream-style corn
115 g tasty cheddar or New Zealand cheshire, grated
salt and pepper

Combine beaten eggs with milk and melted butter. Add breadcrumbs and beat until they have dissolved and mixture is a smooth consistency. Mix in corn and about three-quarters of the grated cheese. Season to taste with salt and pepper. Transfer to a buttered ovenproof dish and top with remaining grated cheese. Place dish in a pan of hot water and bake uncovered for 1 hour at 180°C (350°F).
    Serves 3–4.

Cheese and nut croquettes

3 T grated tasty cheddar
1 C nuts, finely chopped
2 C fresh breadcrumbs
1 small onion, grated
1 T chopped parsley
pinch nutmeg
salt and pepper
1 egg, beaten
milk

Place all ingredients except milk in a bowl and mix
well. Stir in just enough milk to make a stiff paste.
Roll into croquettes, place on a greased oven tray
and bake for 20 minutes at 180°C (350°F).

Serves 3–4.

Desserts, Cakes and Biscuits

Perhaps the greatest achievements of New Zealand home cooking are in the field of cake and biscuit making. Formerly, this skill also extended to those hot steamed and baked puddings so beloved by the English, and throughout the late 19th century and early 20th centuries new versions began to evolve, such as Dominion Pudding, Colonial Pudding, Russell Pudding, Ponsonby Pudding, Marlborough Pudding and Waikari Pudding. Since about the mid-1950s, however, these cannonballs of flour and suet have plummeted out of fashion.

In the early colonial days, rural housewives had little access to town bakeries but the availability of butter, eggs and cream soon became a rich incentive to individual enterprise, and the tradition has been perpetuated by generations of cooks. No doubt the Scottish immigrants, with their long heritage of flour cookery, reinforced the trend, and it is interesting to reflect how cake baking would have developed had a certain Thomas John Edmonds not begun manufacturing baking powder in Christchurch back in 1879. Certainly Victorian New Zealanders, who to some extent observed the English custom of high tea — complete with sandwiches, pies, cold meats, cakes and biscuits — appreciated the practice, as have generations of farm workers for whom a substantial afternoon tea is all but mandatory.

Inevitably, homemade biscuits and cakes have suffered along with heavy puddings as the price of basic ingredients has risen, and even more as women have moved out of the kitchen and into the workforce. Commercial bakers have been quick to fill the gap, turning out imitations of our great national cakes and biscuits. They have produced a million-dollar industry which depends on the illusion that nobody notices the use of margarine instead of butter or mock cream instead of the real thing.

Such travesties are here to stay. But there is still nothing to compare with the satisfaction of truly oven-fresh home baking.

Pavlova

The airy white edifice which New Zealanders affectionately refer to as 'pav' is more than just a national dish; it is an institution, an icon of popular New Zealand culture.

To this day, no country wedding could be complete without pavlova, and while city sophisticates might mock, chances are they still secretly crave this unpretentious meringue cake, topped with whipped cream and sliced kiwifruit.

Though many people actually prefer the solid, chewy texture of a collapsed pavlova, the classic specimen is as ethereal as the famous ballerina after whom it is named. Some people fancy they see a tutu in its colour and shape.

Ironically, Anna Pavlova herself kept to a rigid diet which excluded potatoes, bread and even red meat, let alone such a sumptuous dessert.

The precise origins of pavlova cake are unknown, but the fact that Anna Pavlova toured both Australia and New Zealand in 1926, paved the way for a trans-Tasman controversy over its ownership. This simmered quietly for years, until flaring into a full diplomatic row in 1985 after a Rotoract group in Western Samoa quite innocently asked both the Australian and New Zealand High Commissioners to provide a national dish for a fund-raising evening. When each side discovered the other had decided upon pavlova, their fury resounded in the national press of both countries.

The Australian case rests with an entry in their Macquarie Dictionary claiming the pavlova was invented in 1935 by an Australian chef, Herbert Sachse (1898–1974), and named by Harry Nairn of the Esplanade Hotel, Perth.

However, unfortunately for the Ockers there is plenty of solid evidence that New Zealand came up with a pavlova recipe much earlier. A 1926 cookbook, *Home Cookery for New Zealanders* by E. Futter, lists a recipe for 'Meringue with Fruit Filling'. Although specifying peaches for the topping instead of the now-classic kiwifruit slices, it is clearly recognisable as a pavlova. And in 1933 there is a recipe for 'Meringue Sponge Sandwich or Pavlova Cake' in the third edition of a book simply titled *Cookery* and published by the Dunedin City Gas Department.

Prototypes of pavlova may in fact belong to an older European tradition. In Vienna there is Spanish Wind Cake (Spanische Windtorte), consisting of a meringue base upon which rings of meringue are stacked, forming a hollow shell. This is then filled with whipped cream, nuts, chocolate and berries.

Perhaps the greatest charm of pavlova lies in its simplicity: for the first time, a meringue cake has been taken from the arcane realms of professional patisserie and placed within easy reach of the home cook.

Classic pavlova

4 egg whites
pinch salt
1 C castor sugar
2 t cornflour
1 t vinegar
1 t vanilla essence

Beat egg whites with salt until stiff. Add sugar a tablespoonful at a time, beating after each addition until it is completely dissolved. Sprinkle over cornflour, vinegar and vanilla essence and fold in lightly. Pile onto buttered greaseproof paper sprinkled with cornflour, or straight onto aluminium foil. Do not flatten out the mixture too much if you want a marshmallow centre.

Place in a preheated moderate oven, reduce heat to low, and cook for 1¼ hours. Allow pavlova to cool in oven to avoid cracking. When cool, spread with passionfruit pulp folded into whipped cream and decorate with slices of kiwifruit.

Serves 4–6.

Uncooked pavlova

Although it looks much the same as ordinary pavlova when decorated, this dish has more of a marshmallow than a meringue flavour.

2 T gelatine
½ C lemon juice
½ t vanilla essence
½ C sugar
3 egg whites

Dissolve gelatine in ½ C boiling water, add lemon juice, vanilla essence and sugar and leave to cool. Add to stiffly beaten egg whites and beat together. Pour into a wide, round dish and chill. When set, upend onto a plate and cover with whipped cream and fruit.
Variation: Substitute ½ C pineapple juice for the lemon juice.

Serves 4–6.

Kiwifruit

The kiwifruit, or Chinese gooseberry as it was once known, is a native of China, where it first grew wild and uncultivated on the edges of the forest in the Yangtse Valley. The Chinese name translates as 'monkey peach'.

The first seeds were brought to New Zealand in 1906, probably by a James McGregor, who gave them to a Wanganui nurseryman, James Allison. The first vines fruited in 1910, but commercial planting did not take place until 1937.

The first shipment overseas, to the prestigious London firm of T.J. Poupart in 1952, was put in with a refrigerated consignment of lemons, almost as an afterthought. As luck would have it, the temperature and the length of time taken to reach London meant the fruit arrived there in almost perfect condition. This long-keeping quality was a big reason for its subsequent export success.

In 1953 the firm Turners and Growers Ltd adopted the name kiwifruit for exports to the American market and, for better or for worse, the name has stuck.

Kiwifruit shortcake

Base
90 g butter
120 g sugar
1 egg
1½ C flour
1 t baking powder
1 T milk
Filling
1 T cornflour
4 t sugar
½ C water
juice and rind of 1 lemon
1 t butter
icing sugar
Topping
3 kiwifruit, sliced

Cream butter and sugar and stir in egg. Sift flour and baking powder and add to the mixture alternately with milk. Press into a 20-cm square baking tin and bake for 15 minutes at 180°C (350°F).

Meanwhile make filling by mixing cornflour and sugar with water and lemon juice and rind. Bring to the boil and simmer for 1 minute, then melt in butter. Spread shortcake base with this mixture while shortcake is still warm. Dust with icing sugar and arrange kiwifruit slices over the top. Return to the oven just to heat through. Serve hot.

Serves 8.

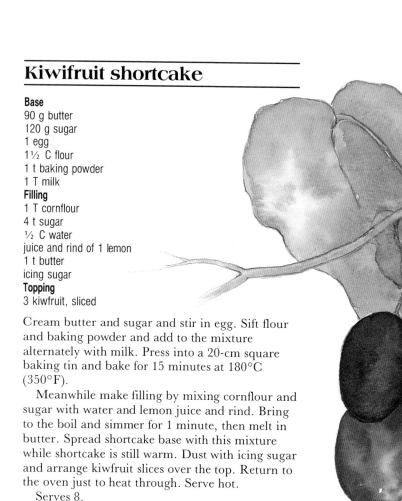

Tamarillos

In most fruit markets of the world the tamarillo would be regarded as a curiosity, for although it is grown in private gardens in a number of tropical countries, only in New Zealand is the fruit cultivated on a commercial scale.

A native of the Andean region of Peru and of southern Brazil, the tamarillo was spread in cultivation after the Spanish conquest. In the 1880s the director of the Botanical Gardens in Jamaica sent seeds to the hill district of India and Sri Lanka, and it was from northern India that seeds were first sent to New Zealand, to D. Hay and Sons, nurserymen of Parnell, Auckland, in 1891. At first only the yellow and purple varieties were grown and it was not until the end of World War I that the now almost universal red variety was bred at Mangere, Auckland.

Commercial production, the first in the world, began in Auckland about this time, but it was only in World War II that production was stepped up, because supplies of tropical fruits were being threatened by the spread of Japanese forces.

For many years in New Zealand the fruit were universally known as 'tree tomatoes'. The name 'tamarillo' officially came into being in January 1967, after almost unanimous agreement among New Zealand growers, who wanted a more exotic-sounding name for export promotion. The origin of the old name is fairly obvious, since the fruit does indeed look like an elongated tomato growing on a tree, and its flesh has a somewhat similar appearance and texture. Tomatoes and tamarillos, in fact, even belong to the same family of plants. The flavour of 'tree tomatoes', however, is vastly different, being more tart, even astringent, as well as sweet and mildly scented.

Tamarillos in port

8 tamarillos
½ C sugar
½ C port wine

Blanch tamarillos for 30 seconds in boiling water. Peel, leaving stalks intact. Place fruit in a saucepan, add sugar and port. Pour over enough water just to cover, then simmer for 20 minutes uncovered. Remove tamarillos. Boil liquid until reduced to a thick syrup and pour over tamarillos when cooled.

Serves 4.

Christmas pudding

The traditions of merrie England die hard in New Zealand. Each Christmas we deck our halls with wreaths of holly (typically the plastic species) and plaster our windows with spray-can snow, as if some quirk of the seasons has landed us back in winter.

This 'white Christmas' fantasy reaches its climax on Christmas Day, when we sit down in the blazing heat to eat roasted ham or turkey followed by a hot stodgy steamed plum pudding.

225 g raisins
225 g currants
170 g sultanas
60 g almonds, chopped
60 g peel, chopped
225 g shredded suet
225 g breadcrumbs
225 g sugar
60 g flour
1 t mixed spice
pinch nutmeg
¼ t salt
4 eggs, beaten
2 T brandy
150 ml milk

Combine all dry ingredients. Beat together eggs, brandy and milk, mix well with dry ingredients and transfer to a greased bowl. Tie greaseproof paper over the top of the bowl, set in a large pot of boiling water, and steam for at least 4 hours. Serve with brandy butter (see recipe below).

Serves 8.

Brandy butter

Another legacy of English cooking, traditionally served with Christmas pudding.

½ C unsalted butter
¾ C brown sugar
1 T brandy (or more)
nutmeg or cinnamon

Cream the butter and brown sugar until smooth. Add the brandy a little at a time, blending in with a wooden spoon. Flavour with nutmeg or cinnamon and chill before serving.

New Zealand Christmas pudding

This cold jelly, which retains many of the ingredients and all the 'atmosphere' of the traditional hot pudding, is better suited to typical Christmas Day temperatures in New Zealand.

125 g raisins
125 g sultanas
75 g currants
75 g prunes
50 g glace cherries, sliced
150 ml sherry
1 T brandy
4 T sugar
rind and juice of 1 lemon
10 g gelatine
whipped cream

Rinse fruit under running water and then bring raisins, sultanas, currants and prunes to the boil in a little water to plump the fruit. Drain. Stone and chop prunes and place back in bowl with cherries. Pour over sherry and brandy and cover tightly to prevent evaporation.

Bring ½ C water to the boil with sugar, lemon juice and rind. Sprinkle over gelatine and stir briskly until dissolved. Add more water to make up 300 ml. Pour over fruit in bowl, mix well and leave to set.

Serve with whipped cream.
Serves 4.

Dominion pudding

Though its inventor is unknown, this pudding appeared soon after New Zealand became a dominion in 1907. It was also known as Anzac pudding for a time after World War I.

60 g butter
1¼ C flour
1 t baking powder
120 g sugar
1 egg
½ C milk
1½ T raisins

Rub butter into flour, add baking powder and sugar. Beat egg and milk together, then stir in to make a batter, taking care to remove all lumps.

Put raisins at the bottom of a greased basin, pour over batter, cover with greaseproof paper and tie with string. Place basin in a pot of boiling water, cover and steam for 1½ hours.

Serves 4.

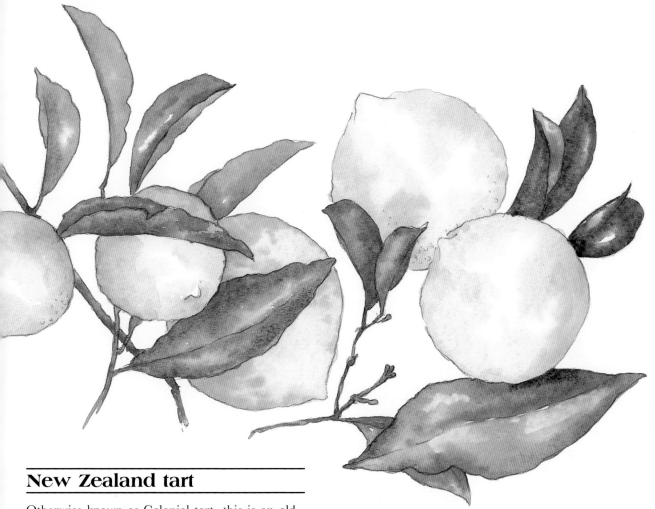

New Zealand tart

Otherwise known as Colonial tart, this is an old New Zealand favourite which crops up time and time again in recipe books compiled by local clubs and organisations.

225 g short pastry
60 g butter
60 g sugar
1 T golden syrup
1 egg, beaten
rind of 1 lemon
juice of 1 lemon
1–2 apples, peeled and grated
30 g coconut
2 T raspberry jam

Line a pie plate with pastry and blind bake for 10 minutes. Cream together butter and sugar, add golden syrup, egg, lemon juice and rind, apple and coconut. Mix well. Spread the pastry shell with jam and pour in the filling.

Bake for 30 minutes at 180°C (350°F) and serve either hot or cold.

Serves 6.

Variation: Some versions suggest using apricot rather than raspberry jam.

New Zealand lemon pie

Base
1 C crushed malt biscuits
¼ C flour
2 T sugar
pinch salt
115 g butter, melted
Filling
150 ml cream
1 can sweetened condensed milk
grated rind of 2 lemons
juice of 3 lemons

Mix together crushed biscuits, flour, sugar and salt. Stir in melted butter. Press into a 20-cm pie dish and bake for 8–10 minutes at 180°C (350°F). Cool and refrigerate.

Whip cream. Slowly stir in condensed milk. Add lemon rind and slowly stir in lemon juice. Pour into pie base and refrigerate.

Serves 6.

Coffee liqueur cream

While making pavlova, add 1½ t instant coffee powder after beating egg whites and before adding salt. Spread cooked pavlova with the following topping:

10 cherries, stoned and halved
sherry
300 ml cream
2 T icing sugar
2 t instant coffee powder
8 pieces preserved ginger, chopped
6 walnuts, chopped

Soak cherries for 2–3 hours in sherry just to cover. Whip cream, add icing sugar and instant coffee powder. Strain sherry from cherries and fold into cream. Spread cream over pavlova and sprinkle with cherries, preserved ginger and walnuts.

Pikelets

Pikelets are to afternoon tea what pavlova is to the wedding breakfast: indispensable. Early Scottish immigrants added baking powder to a recipe known in their home country as 'drop scones' and the result has become a New Zealand specialty.

1 egg
¼ C sugar
½–¾ C milk
1 C flour
1 t baking powder
pinch salt
30 g butter

Beat egg and sugar until thick and add milk. Add sifted flour, baking powder and salt and mix until smooth. The batter should have the consistency of cream. Leave to stand for 30 minutes if possible.

Drop the batter by the tablespoonful into a hot buttered frying pan and brown lightly on both sides, turning when small bubbles appear on the uncooked upper surface. Serve warm with butter and the traditional accompaniments of jam and whipped cream, if desired.

Variations: To make vanilla pikelets, add ½ tsp vanilla essence to the batter. To make orange and date pikelets, reduce quantity of milk to ¼ C and add ¼ C orange juice, grated rind of 1 orange and ⅔ C chopped dates to mixed batter.

Scones

2 C flour
4 level t baking powder
½ t salt
30 g butter
½–¾ C milk

Sift flour, baking powder and salt into a bowl. Rub the butter in with the fingertips until mixture resembles breadcrumbs. Stir in milk and mix to a soft dough. The dough should make your fingers slightly sticky as you handle it.

Pat out dough to about 2 cm thick. Cut into squares or triangles and bake close together on a floured tray at 230°C (450°F) for 10–15 minutes until golden brown.

Serve warm with butter and a sweet or savoury topping, according to taste.
Variations: Add ½ C sultanas, chopped dates or grated cheese to dry ingredients.

Gems

Both gems and the gem irons they are made in are New Zealand inventions. If you are lucky enough to possess a set of the old heavy cast-iron gem irons, do not part with them — they are much better than modern gem irons made with inferior alloys which do not have the same heat-retention qualities.

60 g butter
60 g sugar
1 egg, beaten
225 g flour
1½ t baking powder
⅛ t salt
approx. 1 C milk

Preheat gem irons in a 220°C (425°F) oven. Cream butter and sugar, add beaten egg. Fold in sifted dry ingredients alternately with milk. Remove heated gem irons from the oven, brush the insides with butter and two-thirds fill them with the batter. Bake 10–15 minutes at 220°C (425°F) until risen and brown.

Split and spread with butter. Eat hot or cold.

Sponge sandwich

3 eggs, separated
½ C castor sugar
5 T cornflour
4 t flour
2 t baking powder
Filling
300 ml cream, whipped
raspberry jam

Beat egg whites until stiff, add egg yolks and beat
again until thick. Beat in sugar a tablespoonful at a
time until dissolved. Sift together cornflour, flour
and baking powder and fold into egg white and
sugar.

Pour into two greased and floured 20-cm
sandwich tins. Bake for 15–20 minutes at 190°C
(375°F).

When sponges have cooled, spread one with jam
and cover with whipped cream. Place the other
sponge on top and dust with icing sugar.
Variation: While lamingtons are jealously
guarded as a national dish by the Australians, they
have always been popular in New Zealand as well.
They are made by baking the above sponge in a
square tin. The next day the sponge is cut into
5-cm squares, dipped into thin chocolate icing,
then rolled in desiccated coconut.

Banana cake

90 g butter
¾ C sugar
1 egg, beaten
2 large ripe bananas, mashed
1½ C flour
1 t baking powder
½ t baking soda
4 T milk

Cream butter and sugar and gradually add beaten
egg. Add mashed banana. Sift in flour and baking
powder and mix well. Lastly add baking soda
dissolved in milk.

Pour into a greased tin and bake for 45 minutes
to 1 hour at 180°C (350°F).

Ice with an icing made by mixing equal parts of
cream cheese and icing sugar and adding lemon
juice and rind to taste.
Variation: Make double quantity of batter and
pour into two greased sandwich tins. Bake for 20
minutes. When cool, fill with whipped cream and
sliced bananas.

Sultana cake

225 g butter
1¼ C sugar
3 eggs, beaten
1 t lemon essence
1 t vanilla essence
½ C cold water
2½ C flour
1 t baking powder
¼ t salt
450 g sultanas

Cream butter and sugar, add eggs and lemon and
vanilla essences, then gradually blend in water.
Mix in sifted flour, baking powder and salt. Add
sultanas.

Pour into a greased and floured 20-cm tin. Bake
for 1 hour at 180°C (350°F).

Hokey pokey biscuits

While the related confectionery (see recipe below) is known to British cookery under the name of honeycomb, these biscuits are a New Zealand specialty.

120 g butter
120 g castor sugar
1 T golden syrup
1 T milk
1 t bicarbonate of soda
170 g flour

Cream butter and sugar. Melt together milk and golden syrup and add bicarbonate of soda. Mix well with creamed butter and sugar and stir in sieved flour. Place in teaspoon lots on a greased baking tray, leaving room for expansion. Bake for 10–15 minutes at 180°C (350°F).

Hokey pokey sweets

Bring to the boil 5 T sugar with 2 T golden syrup, stirring slowly but continuously. Boil for 4–5 minutes, stirring from time to time. Remove from heat and quickly stir in 1 t bicarbonate of soda until mixture froths up. Pour into a greased tin and allow to set. Cut up when cold.

Ginger crunch

A plain biscuit base with a creamy, sweet ginger topping; a perennial afternoon tea and cake shop favourite.

225 g flour
120 g brown sugar
1 t baking powder
1 t ground ginger
pinch salt
120 g butter
Icing
30 g butter
2 t golden syrup
120 g icing sugar
2 t ground ginger

Sift dry ingredients and chop or rub in butter until mixture has the consistency of breadcrumbs. Add sugar and mix well. Press into a flat, buttered tin and bake for 25 minutes at 180°C (350°F).

While the base is still warm, pour over icing made as follows: Melt together butter and golden syrup. Beat in icing sugar and ginger. Mix well.

Cut into squares while still warm.

Aotea biscuits

The packed school lunches (as opposed to hot midday meals), which are the norm in New Zealand, have always provided an incentive for regular baking — as have hungry children raiding the biscuit tins after school.

200 g butter
90 g brown sugar
140 g flour
2 heaped T cornflour
1 t baking powder
1 C cornflakes

Cream butter and sugar. Add sifted flour, cornflour, baking powder and fold in cornflakes. Roll into small balls and press with a fork onto a cold, greased oven tray. Bake for 20 minutes at 180°C (350 F).

Slugs

A specialty of the West Coast, these are rather more palatable than their namesakes from the garden.

90 g butter
½ C sugar
1 egg, beaten
1 t vanilla essence
1½ C flour
1½ t baking powder
1 T coconut
dates

Cream butter and sugar. Add beaten egg, vanilla, flour, baking powder and coconut. Roll teaspoon-sized measures in the shape of slugs. Press a date into the belly of each, roll in coconut and bake for 10–15 minutes at 180°C (350°F).

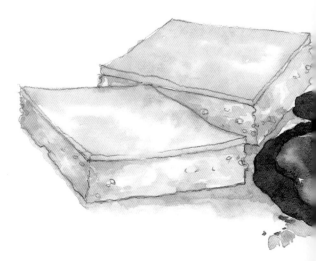

Afghans

Afghans are generally acknowledged to be a New Zealand specialty, although the origin of the name remains a mystery. Biscuit shops abound in Afghanistan, but to the best of my knowledge (and I kept an eye out while I was there) they have nothing quite like these iced cocoa and cornflake-flavoured confections topped with their distinctive walnut halves.

200 g butter
60 g sugar
1 t vanilla essence
170 g flour
30 g cocoa
1 t baking powder
60 g cornflakes, crushed
Icing
30 g cocoa
4 T boiling water
120 g icing sugar
2 t butter
halved walnuts

Beat butter and sugar to a cream, add vanilla essence and mix in sifted flour, cocoa and baking powder. Lastly mix in crushed cornflakes.

Place in teaspoon lots on a greased baking tray and bake for 12–15 minutes at 180°C (350°F).

When cold top with icing made as follows. Stir cocoa to a paste with boiling water and beat in icing sugar and butter. The consistency should be firm enough to coat the back of a spoon. Top each iced afghan with a walnut half.

Variation: To make coffee afghans, substitute cocoa with coffee and chicory essence. Make icing with coffee essence instead of cocoa.

Kiwi crisps

120 g butter
60 g sugar
2 T sweetened condensed milk
60 g dark chocolate, chopped
170 g flour
1 t baking powder

Cream butter and sugar. Add condensed milk, then chocolate, and lastly fold in sifted flour and baking powder. Mix well. Roll into small balls and flatten with a fork onto a greased baking tray. Bake for 20 minutes at 180°C (350°F).

Variation: When the chopped chocolate is omitted, Kiwi crisps become Highlander biscuits. These date back at least as far as 1913, possibly further.

Nutty joys

120 g butter
3 T brown sugar
120 g flour
2 t baking powder
1¼ t cinnamon
⅔ C chopped walnuts
⅔ C sultanas or raisins
½ C milk

Cream butter and sugar, then mix in dry ingredients alternately with milk. Spoon mixture into buttered patty tins and bake at 220°C (425°F) for about 20 minutes.

Anzac biscuits

Perhaps the most famous of the many varieties of biscuit peculiar to New Zealand, these are named after the Australian and New Zealand Army Corps (ANZAC), which fought gallantly and suffered very heavy casualties in Churchill's invasion of the Gallipoli peninsula in 1915.

120 g butter
1 T golden syrup
120 g sugar
120 g flour
120 g rolled oats
120 g desiccated coconut
1 t baking powder

Melt butter and golden syrup together and add sugar to dissolve. Mix with flour, rolled oats, coconut and baking powder. Roll into small balls and flatten onto a greased oven tray.
  Bake for 15 minutes at 160°C (325°F).

Belgian biscuits

Before World War I these were known as German biscuits (presumably introduced by German immigrants). But along with German sausage they underwent a discreet name change as wartime anti-German feeling mounted.

225 g butter
225 g sugar
1 egg
2 T golden syrup
450 g flour
2 t baking powder
5 t cinnamon
3 t ginger
raspberry jam
few drops cochineal

Cream butter and sugar, add egg and golden syrup. Mix in sifted flour, baking powder, cinnamon and ginger. Roll out to 12 mm thick and cut into rounds. Bake for 10 minutes at 180°C (350°F). When cool join together with raspberry jam and ice if desired.

Icing
1½ C icing sugar
2 T water

Mix all ingredients in a saucepan and warm over a low heat until mixture becomes glossy.

Tararua biscuits

These are a New Zealand mountaineer's staple. One of these biscuits even lies buried on the summit of Yerupaja Norte in the Himalayas. This gesture was made by Graeme Dingle, who in 1968 was the first ever to climb the mountain.

  Tararua biscuits must be baked hard to withstand jostling about in a pack. They should be of uniform size so that they can be taped up compactly in a plastic bag. For large quantities it helps to make a biscuit cutter specially for the job.

120 g wholemeal flour
140 g plain flour
140 g rolled oats
60 g oatmeal
170 g sugar
170 g brown sugar
120 g butter
1 T golden syrup
1–2 eggs, beaten
150 ml milk

Combine dry ingredients. Melt together butter and golden syrup and mix in together with eggs and milk. The mixture should be firm and dry.

  Roll out to 12 mm thick and cut into 6-cm squares. Place on a cold, greased oven tray and bake for 45 minutes at 150-180°C (300–350°F).

  Yields about 25 biscuits.

Variations: Extra ingredients which may be added after mixing include chopped dates or raisins, mixed peel, bran, sesame seeds or chopped crystallised ginger.

Beverages

If there is a national drink of New Zealand, it would be beer, and the tradition of brewing in this country is a long one: it was the explorer Captain James Cook who first brewed beer in New Zealand, in 1773, using the foliage of rimu, a native conifer, as flavouring.

While brand-name beers have pride of place in the beverage market, many boutique breweries now produce excellent beers in limited quantities, and home brewing also accounts for around a tenth of all beer consumed. With commercial canned 'brewkits', improved strains of yeast and good quality plastic fermentation vessels now available, the once much-maligned 'home brew' today is usually a palatable and refreshing if potent drink, easily produced for about one-fifth the cost of commercial beer.

Tigger Beer

The inventor of this recipe claims to have made 1,380 litres of beer in the 4 years since he started brewing, but hastens to add that he has had a lot of willing helpers to drink it with him. The beer is so named because it is supposed to 'make you bouncy!'

50 g dried hops
1 kg malt extract
1 kg sugar
1 sachet beer yeast

Boil the hops for 40 minutes in 4 litres of water. Warm the malt for easy pouring and place it and the sugar in a sterilised 20-litre fermentation vessel. Strain the hops infusion through muslin into the fermentation vessel and top up to 20 litres with cold tapwater. Sprinkle yeast on top, cover and keep in a warm place to ferment for 4–5 days until bubbling ceases and specific gravity (measured with a beer hydrometer) is about 1005 or less. Syphon or decant into sterilised bottles with 1 heaped teaspoon of sugar per 750ml bottle, cap and shake to dissolve sugar. Keep in a warm place for a week, then store bottles upright in a cool dark place. This beer is drinkable within 2–3 weeks of bottling but is best after 2–3 months or longer. Chill well and pour carefully into a glass or jug in one continuous movement to avoid disturbing the yeast sediment.

The key to successful home brewing is to be scrupulous about cleanliness (sterilise with boiling water or the sterilant available from brewing-supply shops), check the specific gravity before bottling to avoid burst bottles, and allow the beer to mature as long as possible.

Kiwifruit wine

Kiwifruit make a beautiful dry white wine which retains just a hint of the fruit's bouquet and tangy flavour. This recipe can also be used with many other fruits, such as green gooseberries.

3 kg kiwifruit, peeled
4.5 litres water
1 camden tablet or ½ t metabisulphite
1 kg sugar
1 pkt general purpose wine yeast

Crush kiwifruit in a large bucket and add water, sugar and camden tablet or metabisulphite (this kills off any 'wild' yeasts that might make your wine turn to vinegar.) Cover with a clean tea towel and leave for 24–48 hours. Strain through muslin and transfer to a sterilised fermentation vessel with air lock. Put in a warm place and sprinkle yeast on top. Ferment until hydrometer reading is about 1005 or less and yeast starts to settle (this usually takes a month or more.) Syphon off into clean sterilised 4-litre jar with airlock and allow to complete fermentation and settle until quite clear. Then syphon into sterilised bottles, cap or cork and store in a cool dark place for at least 3 months but preferably a year or more.

Mint lemonade

Cordials with artificial colouring and flavouring used to be the standard non-alcoholic drink, but are becoming supplanted by more healthy drinks such as fruit juice or cordials made from real fruit. This is a light, refreshing cordial ideal for a hot day.

1½ C sugar
4 sprigs mint, plus extra for garnish
3 lemons
1 t citric acid
½ t lemon essence

Place sugar and 2 cups of water in a saucepan and heat until sugar has dissolved. Add mint, boil for 10 minutes, then take off the heat and add the juice of the 3 lemons. Strain. Add citric acid and lemon essence, cool and bottle.

To drink, dilute 1:4 with cold water and add a slice of lemon and sprig of mint.

Index